Dealing With Dad

Teens Write About Their Fathers

By Youth Communication

Edited by Virginia Vitzthum

YOUTH
COMMUNICATION
True Stories by Teens

Dealing With Dad

EXECUTIVE EDITORS
Keith Hefner and Laura Longhine

CONTRIBUTING EDITORS
Clarence Haynes, Hope Vanderberg, Andrea Estepa, Nora McCarthy,
Tamar Rothenberg, Virginia Vitzthum, Duffie Cohen, Katia Hetter,
Kendra Hurley, and Phillip Kay

LAYOUT & DESIGN
Efrain Reyes, Jr. and Jeff Faerber

COVER ART
Ian P. Jones / YC Art Dept.

For reprint information, please contact Youth Communication.

ISBN 978-1-935552-27-7

Second, Expanded Edition

Printed in the United States of America

Youth Communication ®
New York, New York
www.youthcomm.org

Catalog Item #YD32-1

Table of Contents

Contents

Some POPS Are Hanging In

> The POPS Program in Harlem helps young African-
> American and Latino fathers to reunite and connect
> with their children.

Saying Goodbye to My Superman

> When Griffin's father is dying from AIDS, he finally
> opens up to his son.

My Father, My Friend

> People often mistake Macario and his dad for friends
> rather than father and son, but they're not really mis-
> taken: the two share many interests and value their
> time together.

Meeting the Invisible Man

> At age 15, Athena visits her long-absent father, who
> lives in Greece. They have a wonderful summer, but it
> doesn't last.

Tracing My Family Tree

> Hazak writes about his father's efforts to research their
> family's history.

Using the Book

Introduction

Studies show that children who grow up with their fathers around tend to do better in school and are less likely to develop a drug or alcohol problem or get into other trouble. But the research doesn't answer some more basic questions: What is a teenager missing if her father is gone or abuses her? What is a father supposed to provide his son? What does a good dad add to his children's lives? Can teenagers really only get those things from a father?

The stories in this book tackle those questions and more. Dina Spanbock and Daniela Catillo both discover that the path to their father's heart is through his interests. Dina and her dad share a love of music, and Daniela becomes a fan of foreign films to get close to her father.

Listening to a CD of her father's, Dina thinks about all the music he enjoyed before she was born. She writes, "It made me realize that he wasn't just my father, but a person who had his own life and everything that came along with it, including a childhood. We were both individuals with our own pasts and interests. We had this connection as people now, not just as father and daughter."

Similarly, Macario DeLaCruz feels more like a friend than a son to his dad (they don't live together). He likes that people mistake them for brothers or friends and that they say goodbye with a fist pound, not a kiss. Dina, Daniela, Macario, and other writers here reveal how children hunger to hear details of their fathers' lives and develop a special relationship with them, even when they live apart.

When fathers don't live up to their roles, kids must decide how to balance their longing for a relationship with the need to protect themselves. In "I Think These Drugs Are Daddy's," for example, the narrator is devastated when it becomes clear that her father, whom she has always been closest to, is using crack.

The narrator's sister eventually gives up on their dad, "for not being there financially and for not being the kind of father she can talk to her friends about."

But the writer isn't willing to let him go. To her, what matters most is that he's always made an effort to stay involved in her life, and to listen to and encourage her. "I remain faithful to my dad because he has remained faithful and loyal to me," she concludes.

Other writers who discover that they can't count on their fathers try to accept the loss and move on—and even use it to guide themselves. Onician Wood writes of the father who abandoned him and his mother, "There was no use in hating him because he's my father. And in a backwards way, he's had the biggest impact on my view of life. I set standards for myself by rebelling against what he represents to me, which is a deadbeat, a coward, a cheater." After cutting school to get her father's attention, Natalie Olivero switches schools and applies herself, realizing, "I'm trying to not hurt myself anymore just because my father has hurt me."

Of course, some of the writers here are lucky enough to live with their role models. Stephen Simpson wants to be like his father because of "the way he carries himself and treats his children, and the way he lives his life." He's equally grateful for his discipline. "My father will always pull us aside if we're falling off track. To me, that shows that he cares about us, because if he didn't, he wouldn't bother to say anything."

But overall, it's striking how few positive fathers appear in this book. This is, unfortunately, an accurate reflection on the experiences of the teens in our program, the majority of whom are New York City teens of color. It also reflects the larger trend of fatherless-ness in America, particularly in minority communities. Roughly 65% of black families and 35% of Latino families are now led by a single parent (and that single parent is usually a mother, not a father). What these stories show is how teens who are missing a good father can deal with their emotions and find alternative role models and supports for themselves.

Whether they find it in their biological dad, step-dad, foster dad, adoptive dad, or teacher, mentor, or friend, all of these writers long for the same things: someone who will encourage, talk, listen, guide, and, most of all, be there.

In the following stories, names have been changed: *I Think These Drugs Are Daddy's; Not My Idea of a Father;* and *The Guy I Call My Dad.*

Sara Goldys

Father Lessons

By Otis Hampton

Lesson One: Abandonment

My biological parents left me at St. Mary's Hospital for Children in Queens, New York, when I was 2 years old. I was later told that they left me there because they could no longer take care of me, though they did keep my older brother and my little sister. I was sure my real parents would come back for me. But as months and then years went by with no visit from them, I grew more confused, and raged at the nurses and the other kids.

When I was about 4, a woman I didn't know started visiting the room I shared with a lot of other kids. She watched us from the doorway a few times, and then one day she introduced herself. "Hello, Otis. My name is Juanita and I'm going to be your mom."

I was confused. Because I was either violent or withdrawn, adults tended not to talk to me for very long. I wondered if this lady was going to take me someplace where my real mom would pick me up.

Juanita took me out of the hospital and brought me home with her. That's when I met her husband, Leroy Hampton. Unfortunately he was very sick, so I had to go back to St. Mary's for a while. But in 1996, I came back to live with them as their foster child. I met their biological son, Brian, and a younger boy they were already fostering named Denzel.

My only memory of my birth parents is a short glimpse of my biological father. He came to visit me at the Hamptons' house when I was 6. I didn't know how to feel because I barely knew him. He took me out to eat and he even had a conversation with my then-foster parents. They all seemed pretty close, so I assumed my father was back in my life.

I never saw him or anyone else from my birth family again.

Leroy, however, took over when I came back in 1996 and decided to be the man that my father apparently couldn't be. He was fair, and his parenting methods were basic. He'd tell me, "Go to school, do your homework, eat dinner, take a shower, watch a little TV, and go to bed by 9 so that you can get up for school in the morning."

As long as I did what Leroy told me, things went smoothly—for the first time in my life. It was easier to follow rules set by someone who cared for me and who acknowledged when I did well. I began to like him. I'd never had a true father figure before Leroy. I started to call him "Dad" after I asked my mother what his name was. She said, "His name's Leroy and he is going to be your father." After a few months, I realized I hadn't thought about my biological dad since I'd moved there (until he turned up for that one visit).

Leroy and I began to do fun things together. We would watch things on TV as a family, even cartoons. He showed me how to program a VCR when I wanted to watch a movie. There was even one fun time where I went on a bowling trip with my 1st grade class. I saw my dad and his friends, just by coincidence; they also went bowling on Thursdays. I was excited because he was watching my first game and he was proud of me, even though I sucked.

Leroy also taught me how to write neatly. With his hand guiding me, I learned to write my name straight across the lines instead of diagonally, all over the paper. "Watch what I do," he would tell me before instructing me to repeat his action. "Is that good?" I'd ask. "Not bad. Keep it up, Otis," he'd say. Then we moved on to sentences like "I love my Dad." I still have neat handwriting and I still love to write.

Feeling accepted and safe allowed me to think more clearly. In the hospital, I'd heard nurses refer to me as a troublemaker, but Juanita and Leroy bragged to their friends about how smart I was. I thought (correctly) that my biological parents were never going to return, so after several months, I accepted the Hamptons as a permanent replacement.

Feeling accepted and safe allowed me to think more clearly.

My dad and I also had serious talks about things such as education, relationships with girls, and even becoming a father myself one day. He often told me, "You can be anything you want to be as long as you have a good education."

With great patience, he taught me right from wrong. If I misbehaved in school, of course he would get mad, but he would take the time to talk to me about what I did wrong and how I could prevent it from happening again. Or, if I had a fight with my little brother, he was right there to instruct and guide us.

My dad also taught me to set an example for Denzel. He'd say, "Otis, you're the man of the house, and it's your responsibility to keep Denzel out of trouble and teach him right from wrong." Whatever my dad taught me I tried to pass on to Denzel, so I also got a few early lessons in fatherhood.

Then, just before my 8th birthday, Leroy had a stroke and died. I not only lost a father, I lost my best friend.

Death was new to me. I'd never seen grown-ups cry before. They kept telling me it was OK to cry and that I should talk about it, but I shut down completely. I stopped talking to my family and to my friends at school. I didn't understand why he died and I didn't understand why I pushed everyone away.

My little brother seemed afraid of me when I was silent, but about a week after the funeral, he got up the courage to ask from my bedroom's doorway, "Are you all right, Otis?" I said, "Yes," and he was so happy he ran into my room and hugged me.

After my father's death, other men gave me advice over the years. I have many uncles in my adoptive family, including one who always adored me. We call him "Coffee." He had strong opinions about my future: "Otis, you should be a doctor or else study law." Back when Johnnie Cochran was alive, Coffee was always talking about how smart he was.

But even though I want to be a writer and Coffee would rather I became a lawyer or doctor, I still believe Coffee and the rest of my family would be glad to see me doing anything I love. They all know how happy I was as a child and how torn apart I was when Dad died. Coffee, my mother Juanita, Denzel, and other relatives want to see me as happy as I was when I was a child.

There are times when they do see me happy, like if I'm shooting hoops with Denzel or making them laugh, and there are times when I want to be alone, which they usually understand.

I didn't have Leroy for long enough, but I was lucky he was such a good father. He taught me to be proud of things I worked hard at, but also to be humble. The point was not to show off, but to be proud of myself. His early encouragement helped steer me toward being a writer, but that won't be for glory or fame. As a writer, I'll be out there in the future doing what I love, which is glory enough.

Sometimes it was hard to apply my dad's lessons after he died because I wasn't a man yet. I was still a child. There were times I was bullied and I wished that my dad was still around to help resolve the situation. I would look up at the sky and talk to him and God as if they were both listening. He always encouraged resolving things peacefully, and that's what I try to do now.

I've had a mother, and she's provided food, clothes and shelter, love, encouragement, and an understanding of right and wrong. But there are times when I need a father to talk to and the fact that my father is gone still fills me with sadness every day.

If my dad were still around in my adolescence, I guess I wouldn't feel like my family was lopsided, with half the parents missing. At the very least, I would've had someone to talk

I would look up at the sky and talk to my dad and God as if they were both listening.

to and listen to me when I felt that no one else would or cared to. My dad was steadier and less emotional than my mom. I guess I would also have better control of my emotions in general, because much of my sadness and anger comes from his early death.

I'm sure he would be proud of all that I've accomplished and all I plan to accomplish in the near future. If he were still alive today, I would tell him of my appreciation for all that he's done for me and I'd thank him for the guidance that I've needed since I was given up for adoption.

Otis was 18 when he wrote this story.
He went on to attend college.

Daniela Castillo

How I Learned to Love My Stepdad

By Angelis Ulloa

My mom came to the United States from the Dominican Republic when I was very small. I stayed behind with my aunt. Finally, when I was 9, my mom sent for me. There were a lot of new things I had to get used to living here. One of them was having a stepfather.

When I arrived in the U.S., my mom told me that in five more days I would meet her husband. She had told me something about him before but I hadn't really paid attention. At that age, fun was the only thing on my mind.

A few days later I was coming through the living room, and standing there was a tall man with light skin, a black mustache, and black hair. He looked like he lifted weights and had a big smile on his face. When I saw him I thought he must be an uncle

I hadn't met yet. But he was my stepfather.

My mother and I moved out of the place where we had been staying and into my stepfather's apartment. I was very worried since I had never lived with a man around the house. I didn't know what to expect.

Each day that went by I would observe him. Like when we used to sit down to eat dinner, I always looked at him to see his reaction. Did he like the food my mom cooked? He used to notice that I was looking at him, and he always said that the food was good. Sometimes when he caught me looking, he would ask me if there was anything wrong. I guess I just wasn't used to eating with a man around.

I could tell that my stepdad really wanted me to like him. He tried his best to convince me that he was a great guy. When I did something wrong, he would try to help me deal with it, instead of screaming at me the way my mom did. He would ask me if I needed anything at all, like school supplies or clothing. He would take me shopping and buy me things I never thought about having, like fashionable clothes. I felt so good about the ways he would help me and try to please me.

I would observe my new stepfather to see his reaction to my mom's cooking.

As I got older, we became even closer, so close I began to call him Dad. He would always notice when there was something wrong with me. Like when I first arrived in the United States, there were people who used to make fun of me since I didn't know any English. That hurt my feelings. My stepdad would always notice when there was something wrong and help me through those bad times.

He also helped my relationship with my mother. When I was 15, I wanted to wear makeup and it was hard to tell my mom since she was so strict with me. She always said that girls shouldn't wear makeup until they graduate from high school.

Dealing With Dad

My mom was brought up in a very strict family and never wore makeup herself until she was 20. There were times I felt like telling her that those days were gone, but if I had done that she would had have slapped me around until she felt like stopping. I told my stepdad and he told me I should talk to her but he would do what he could. He tried to give my mom clues about it. He told her I would look much better with a little bit of lipstick on.

It took her a long time to start getting the clues, but when she figured it out she was furious. She said I wanted to wear makeup because I had a boyfriend and that my friends were a bad influence. A while later, I was cleaning and my mom started saying that I did not know how to clean, all I knew how to do was think about guys and makeup.

The situation got sick. My stepdad noticed so he took my mom and me and sat us down to talk nice and calm. Everything got worked out, and I can wear a little makeup now. He has also convinced my mom that it's OK for guys to call me. These things would not have been possible without my stepdad. For all these reasons, I have learned to love my stepdad as a real father. He has really helped me solve a lot of my problems and shown me how to be open to people.

Angelis was 15 when she wrote this story.

Julieth Riano

Suddenly, My Dad Is a Question Mark

By Natalie Kozakiewicz

One day in December, I went to my foster care agency to get copies of my parents' death certificates, which I needed for college financial aid applications. I left there a different person. In a tiny, crowded room, I found out that the angry, drunken man I thought was my father probably wasn't. And everything I believed about who I was and where I came from was turned upside down.

My "dad" died of cancer when I was 10. Two years later my mom died too, and my sister and I went into foster care. It was one of my foster care caseworkers who asked me in my agency that day: "Who was 'Cywinski?' Your mom has that as her last name on her death certificate."

I knew that my mom had once been married to a guy named

John Cywinski. But I always assumed she divorced him and married Michael Orbes, the guy who'd been around as long as I could remember. He's who I thought was my father.

I never really loved him. When I was 4, he threw a can of Budweiser at my mom. The can rolled under her shoe and my mom broke her leg. Officially, my mom died of a heart attack, but it didn't help that her broken leg never healed.

"Does that mean my mom was always married to John Cywinski and never to Michael Orbes?" I asked my caseworker.

"Most likely, yes," he said.

This brought up something that I had always wondered about. "Why does my sister have Orbes as a last name and I don't?" I asked. "Is it possible that Michael Orbes is not my father?"

"There's more of a chance that Cywinski might be your father than Orbes," he said.

When my caseworker said this, I knew it was true. I was shocked, and flooded with all kinds of confusing questions and fears. Could I really have a live father out there somewhere? If Michael wasn't my dad, did that mean that this guy John Cywinski was my father? Or was somebody else my dad?

I found out that the angry, drunken man I thought was my father probably wasn't.

And what about my identity as an orphan? I always felt I was different from other kids in the system who were abandoned by their fathers or didn't even know their fathers' names. Sure, my mom and dad were alcoholics, but they didn't abandon me—they died. If my dad had left me, I wasn't an orphan anymore. I was just another ghetto child in foster care who never knew her father.

So much of my past is a mystery to me because there was never anyone to explain things or answer my questions. When my mother was alive, she was an alcoholic and disabled. Michael was sick, too, missing his hair from cancer and usually locked up in his room drunk. I had to make sense out of things as best I could.

My mom had told me she'd left Ohio to escape John Cywinski, so right after the meeting I went to a computer and looked up "John Cywinski" in Ohio. There were a lot, and I wrote down some of their locations. Then I thought, "If Cywinski is my father, I might not be so happy."

My mom told me Cywinski had abused her. When I was about 11 and we were living in Brooklyn, New York, my mom got a threatening call from him that terrified her. She piled chairs in front of the door of the tiny one-bedroom apartment where we lived with my sister and grandmother. My mom grabbed a big kitchen knife and said she'd be ready for him if he came, but he never did. When I think of the name "John Cywinski," I remember being frightened and feeling, "This is serious."

What was he after? I didn't know then, and thought maybe my mom had overreacted. Now I wondered if Cywinski wanted to see me. Could my mom have gotten pregnant by him in Ohio before having me in New York? If he was my dad, did he know I existed?

It was getting late and I decided not to do anything with all the John Cywinskis I found on the Internet. For the moment, I would just leave things alone. But on the train home that evening, I wrote out possibilities and questions on a little piece of paper. I wanted to understand this mix-up.

This wasn't the first surprise I'd had over my identity and name. When I was 10, my Social Security card came in the mail and my mom told me to sign it using the name "Tabitha." This surprised me, because I grew up being called Natalie, the name on all my school records. When I asked my mom why I shouldn't sign my name on my Social Security card, she said Natalie wasn't my real name! Michael, she explained, didn't like the name "Tabitha," so they gave me a new one when I was a baby!

On my birth certificate, there was no name at all under

"father." So who was my father? I was really hyped about this mystery and called up my sister, Cynthia, who is 18 months younger than I am. I started to tell her how I found out we might not have the same fathers.

"No, no, that's not true," she said. Cynthia got really quiet.

I told her I had my reasons for believing it, but she wouldn't listen. Then I realized my exciting news might bother her. If Michael wasn't my dad, she might feel even more alone because she would be the only one to lose both parents. Maybe it upset her to find out she didn't have a full-blooded sister.

I didn't think it mattered much since we've been there for each other all our lives. Same father or not, Cynthia is still my sister. I love her the same whether we're related 100%, 50% or 0%! But I couldn't talk to her about this because she didn't want to hear it.

I realized that I had a fantasy of who I wanted my father to be. After Michael died, my mom had a boyfriend named Donnie with dirty blonde hair and brown eyes like me. He had a real job, and always helped out with groceries or brought us take-out food during the weekends. He stopped by on our birthdays and went to dinner parties that my mom organized at restaurants. After my mother died, he stayed in touch for while, bringing us presents and visiting. He felt so much more like a father than Michael.

I realized that I had a fantasy of who I wanted my father to be.

Finding out if I had a father, I realized, was a really big deal. I thought about steps I could take to find out the truth. For instance, my sister and I have a family friend, Monika, who said she is keeping a secret from Cynthia and me until she feels we're old enough to understand.

She has dropped a lot of hints about how my sister Cynthia and I don't look alike. I could ask Monika to tell me something about my dad. She might know because she and my mom used to talk about private, serious things, things my mother never talked to me about. I could also ask Cynthia to take a DNA test with me to find out if we are full-blooded sisters. But I don't want to ask her since she wants to ignore the whole thing.

Not long ago, I thought about all the pros and cons of trying to solve this mystery. The main reason I want to meet my father (if I have one) is to find out more about my mother. I want to know how my father met my mother, and what she was like, because she died before I got to know her well. If I found out I had a living father, he could tell me things about my mom I never knew, like what kind of jobs she held, whether he was in love with her, or if he was married to her when I was made.

My father is just a big question mark to me, but I'm curious about my mom because she seems more real and I miss her. I have memories of her in her wheelchair cooking us chicken in red sauce and hugging us before we went to school. She felt chubby and warm when her arms went around me.

If my father turned out to be John Cywinski, I'd want to know about his family background and his other relatives, who would be my relatives, too. My mom kept a picture of him with his first daughter, who was older than me. If Cywinski was my dad, that girl would be my half-sister. And if Cywinski wasn't my dad, maybe I could turn out to have a nice father. I wonder what that might be like.

I don't think it would bother me if it turns out that my real father is dead. Ever since I was 10 I thought I had a dead father, so that would be nothing new. Even if he turned out to be alive and I didn't like him, it wouldn't matter: I have plenty of people who have been there, and are here, for me.

But then I thought of the cons: I don't want to make my sister feel even more alone because she can't share the loss of both parents with me anymore. And if Cywinski is my dad and turns out to be alive, he might terrify me like he terrified my mom. Being around a violent man would make my life a lot more complicated. That I don't need.

Also, I don't put much stock in biological relationships. I consider two other girls I know my sisters, even though we're not related. Because Michael was only focused on alcohol, I never really had a father in the first place. I'm so used to not having a dad, I don't really know what I'd do with one.

Since I had that conversation with my caseworker a few months ago, I've realized I'm not so hyped about finding out more—not right now at least. I have more serious priorities, such as my spring semester grades, summer classes, and finding a summer job. Maybe in the future, when I get these things done, I'll see if I really need to solve the mystery of my last name.

Natalie was 18 when she wrote this story. She went on to college and graduate school, studying anthropology.

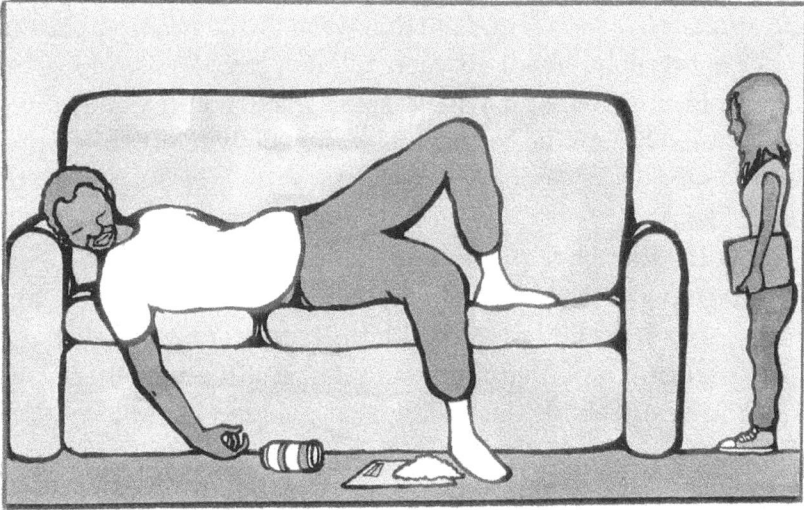

Garnal Jones

I Think These Drugs Are Daddy's

By Anonymous

When I was 9, my mother told me that she and my father had been crack addicts for about two years, before my two older sisters and I were born. She said smoking crack was very common back in the '80s.

Hearing that my parents had been crackheads came as a surprise to me. The crackheads I saw in my community stank, looked dirty, and begged for money. I couldn't imagine my parents this way. They had an apartment together, they both worked, and they were always clean. But I felt glad that my mother told me, because it was better than hearing it from someone else.

My mother told me she got off drugs by going to rehab and Narcotics Anonymous and getting support from counselors and family members. She said my dad went his own way, so I figured he used a different method to quit than my mom had. Unfortunately, I soon found out that wasn't what my mom meant.

One afternoon about six months later, my 12-year-old sister came into our bedroom with a small glass bottle, about three inches tall, with a blue cap. There was some type of white powder in it and I was super curious. "Tyleah, where'd you get this from?" I asked.

"Daddy's drawer. You know he does drugs," she said.

I looked at the bottle in amazement. The white powder was drugs! My sister and I played with the bottle for a while, looking at it closely, twirling it around and passing it to each other.

"You really think this belongs to Daddy? Or Mommy?" I asked her. I wanted so badly for it to belong to someone besides my father, even if that person was my mother. It would have been easier to deal with this kind of betrayal from my mom, because I trusted my dad so much.

My father had always lived with us and been a big part of my life. He picked me up from school, and often drove the family to Coney Island. Best of all, on nice days, Dad would sit me on his lap and let me steer the car down alleyways and empty streets. That made me feel close to him and like he trusted me as much as I trusted him.

That trust was important to me, because I never felt my mother and I had any trust between us. Everything I told her, whether it was about a boy I liked or problems at school, she'd tell her friends or use against me in arguments. We never saw eye to eye on anything—what I should wear, what sport I should play, or who I should be friends with. I felt she wanted to create me, instead of letting me become my own person. I hated this, so I hid everything from her.

But Dad was different. He'd listen closely to my thoughts, looking into my eyes and nodding his head, trying to understand me. This made me feel important and loved by my father, something a lot of my peers couldn't relate to. Most of them came from single-mom homes and didn't have close bonds with their fathers.

So I was crushed when my sister said, "I think these drugs are Daddy's. He be sleepin' with his eyes almost open and he be havin' that white stuff in his nose all the time." I was shocked. My dad had always told me the white stuff was from eating powdered doughnuts, and I'd believed him.

For a long time after that I didn't let myself think about it. I just hoped my sister was wrong. But when I was 11 or 12 I began to see movies about drugs, like *New Jack City*. I saw characters in those movies nodding off from crack, and realized I often saw my dad nodding off that way.

I was scared because those movies always had bad endings like death or jail. I wondered if Daddy would have a bad ending too. I couldn't bring myself to talk to him about it, because I was afraid he'd get upset and because I just didn't want to think about it. So I kept pretending it wasn't happening.

My parents both worked, but I guess my dad wasn't bringing in enough money to support his habit and help out with the bills. I heard my mother and him go back and forth about money all the time.

One night when I was about 13, I was watching TV with my sister when I heard my parents having another money argument. This one was different, though. It sounded louder and angrier, and for the first time my mom screamed out loud about my dad's drug addiction.

"I'm tired of this, Oscar!" she yelled. "You can't stay here and use drugs anymore. I won't allow my children to be around you this way!"

"Those are my kids too! I do more for you than you would ever do for yourself," my father said.

"Those drugs robbed you of your sense, and even worse, my best friend. I don't even know who you are anymore. Oscar, you have to leave, for good."

When I heard this I felt hurt. If my father left, what would happen to our bond? I knew he would still come to visit, but things wouldn't be the same. My father came to my room. My sister and I acted like we hadn't heard anything, continuing to stare at the TV. "Kids, I'm leaving. See ya'll later," he said calmly.

"Where you going, Daddy?" I asked.

"For a walk."

Daddy didn't come back for a month. My mom later told me that he'd gone to live in a shelter. I guess he didn't tell me because he knew I'd hate to see him in there.

I knew that if I asked, my dad would tell me the truth. So I didn't ask.

After that month he started coming to visit us twice a week for an hour or two. My mom acted like he wasn't there, but that never stopped him from asking me how my day was, then telling me to stay and watch TV with him. We didn't talk much, but being with him for those short visits was important to me. For just a little while, it felt like old times again.

One evening about a year later, when I was a freshman in high school, my mom, sister, and I were watching *American Idol* when the phone rang. "Hello?" my mom said. "Yes, this is she. Kings County? For what?"

She got off the phone and told us that my father was in the intensive care unit on a respirator. When I heard I.C.U., I became highly alarmed. I wanted to see him immediately. Although I didn't know why Dad was in the hospital, I somehow knew it had to do with his drug addiction.

"What are we waiting for? Let's go to the hospital!" I said. But my mother told me she wanted to wait a couple of days because she didn't want me to see him that way.

I went to my room and listened to music to try to soothe the thoughts that were now haunting me. I thought my father was going to die. I was scared to see him, but after three days I decided to go there on my own. I wanted to be supportive, like I knew he would be for me.

It was scary. Seeing the machine breathing for him was like watching a scene from a movie. He had tubes down his throat and his chest was going up and down. He woke up when I came in, looked at me with wide eyes and smiled. But I began to cry. He tried to say something but couldn't. He tried and tried until mucus suddenly began coming from his nose.

I got really scared and called out for the nurse. As she walked slowly toward the room, I yelled, "Hurry up, something is wrong with him! What the hell are you walking slow for?"

"Miss, you cannot make all this noise. This is the intensive care unit," she said. I cursed at her and stormed away before she could kick me out. I was frustrated not only with the nurse, but with my dad's condition. Why couldn't he just leave the drugs alone?

A couple of days later when Dad was finally off the respirator and able to speak, he told me he'd been trying to say, "I love you." It made me feel important that despite his condition, he made sure to let me know how much he loved me. Even when he couldn't breathe on his own, he still wanted to reassure me of his love.

My father finally recovered after two months and moved in with his sister in Queens. The doctors said that the drugs had temporarily stopped his breathing. I was hoping this was his wake-up call, but his drug addiction continued.

I still never said anything to him about his drug abuse, though, out of respect and a little bit of fear of what he would say. I didn't want to nag him about using, because I knew that's what everyone else did to him. I thought it would upset him and he might not come over as much and spend time with me. I just wanted him to be peaceful, and I didn't want our relationship to change.

About six months after my dad got discharged from the hospital, I came home from school one day and the house smelled like a homeless person. I walked in to find Daddy on the couch smoking a cigarette. "Hey Larissa!" he called out.

"Hi Daddy." I jumped into his arms and realized the homeless person smell was coming from him. I was worried. What if he was really homeless? I knew that if I asked, he would tell me the truth. So I didn't ask.

"Need some money?" he asked.

"Nope, already got enough," I answered. We sat and talked about a whole bunch of stuff: school, and different jobs that interested us, like being actors and flight attendants. He put his arm around me and the smell got worse. But I acted as if it didn't bother me. Our conversation was more important. Sometimes when he came over he was high and nodding off. But he didn't

My sister has disowned my father, but I remain faithful to him because he has remained faithful and loyal to me.

seem high this time. He sat up straight and paid close attention to our conversation.

My dad still visits me every week. He tells me how proud he is of my accomplishments and that he's planning to get his own place in Brooklyn soon and wants me to visit often. But we never talk about his drug use.

Nowadays, Dad looks like the crackheads I see in my community. Every day I hope he doesn't overdose and die, and sometimes I think only my faith will keep him alive.

If I had the heart to talk to my dad about it, I would ask him what his childhood was like, because I believe a person's childhood affects their adult life. I've never heard my dad speak about what happened to him growing up, and I wonder if any of it would give me a clue about why he's addicted to drugs now.

I would also tell my dad that his drug abuse makes me feel neglected and at times like he doesn't care for me. I'd tell him that it enrages me that when he took those drugs and almost died, he didn't think about me or what I would go through if he died. I felt like he didn't care about my feelings or life, only his pleasure.

But while my dad has shown me something I never want to become, he has also shown me what it means to have love and support for someone, no matter what. My sister Tyleah has disowned my father for not being there financially and for not being the kind of father she can talk to her friends about. She claims she doesn't have a father, like he never existed. But to me, disowning a parent would be like disowning your arm, because your parents are a part of you.

Most of all, I remain faithful to my dad because he has remained faithful and loyal to me. Throughout all of his drug use, my dad has always managed to stop by and check up on me. He has always stayed interested in my activities and school. He encourages me to finish school and stay focused. When I think of my dad, I don't think of a drug abuser. I think of how much of a good father he has been to me.

The author was in high school when she wrote this story.
She later attended college.

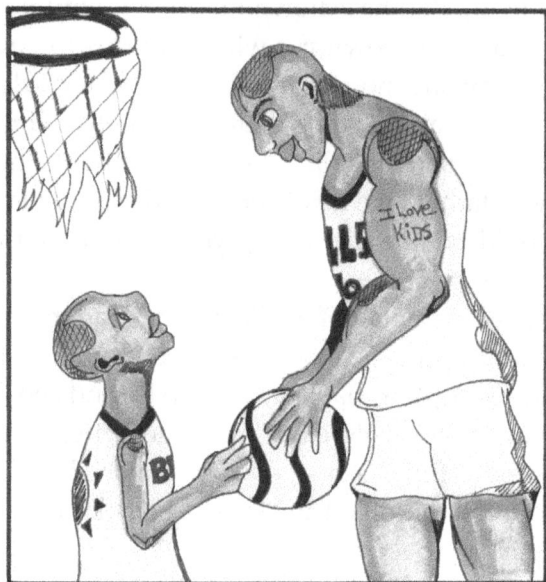

Luis Pabon

Just the Two of Us

By Stephen Simpson

The local park. A father and son playing basketball.

If you're watching from the sidelines, you can feel the competitiveness. The hard fouls, the tight defense, the bragging with each basket. Even though you're not playing, the rivalry is there with you.

What's the score? 30-28. One basket could end the game.

"It's over, Dad, this is my game."

"We'll see, just shoot the ball."

The son shoots and misses, and the father makes an easy put-back to tie the score at 30-30. "Game's 34 now," the father says with an "I'm gonna win" attitude. Two baskets later, game over; the father wins. "Don't worry, Stephen, someday you'll beat me," he says with a laugh to his teary-eyed companion. His words are followed by a hug and an ice cream to enjoy on the way home.

This is an everyday scene, two guys playing basketball. Except this bond is much deeper. This is the relationship I share with the only man I love: my father. I believe that every boy or young man deserves a male role model or influence in his life. My role model goes by the name of Frederick Simpson Sr. I consider it a privilege to share a relationship with him, especially since some young men grow up and never meet or see their fathers.

I also talk with my mother, but we don't have that "guy" connection I have with my father, you know?

I always tell my father that I want to be like him because of the way he carries himself and treats his children, and the way he lives his life. He shows the same love to my friends that don't have fathers, that he shows me.

Ever since I can remember, my father has taken time out to be with me, my brother, and my sister. Even though he works two jobs, he doesn't let this interfere with the family. He does this because he never had a tight relationship with his father, so he tries to give us all the love and attention we need.

I also talk with my mother, but we don't have that "guy" connection I have with my father, you know? Still, my mother has also influenced me in ways my father can't. She teaches me etiquette because she wants me to be a gentleman (which I am). She teaches how to treat women because (come on, you know why!). Most of all, she teaches me independence, because following the crowd almost never pays off. I think she's responsible for the softer, quieter side of me.

I love my parents for instilling their wisdom in me, and for letting me know clearly what is right and wrong. My parents laid down the laws for our house a long time ago. Their rules are:

1. They are the authority (like it or not).
2. Don't ever be afraid to bring anything to them.
3. Go to school and do well.

(There are others, but I don't want to write a book.)

I know my parents have lived longer and seen it all, so they usually have the answers for my problems. And my father will always pull us (me, my brother, sister, or friends) aside if we're falling off track. To me, that shows that he cares about us, because if he didn't, he wouldn't bother to say anything.

If I am making my relationship with my parents seem perfect, I'm not trying to. I have had quite a few fallings out with my folks. For example, when I began my sophomore year of high school, just about all I did was cut class. We argued a lot over my report card grades that year. And my parents get mad when my attitude shows up in a conversation, or when I do something wrong and I don't want to admit it.

My dad was smart enough to do anything, but no one encouraged him to do it.

But I guess I trust that my parents are right about most things because I saw what happened to my brother when he stopped listening to them. My brother was "numero uno" in our house for years, but he decided that he wanted to be with his friends more than his family. In high school he became rebellious and didn't listen to our parents anymore. He ended up dropping out of high school and getting kicked out of the house.

I try to heed my parents' words because I learned at a young age to trust their advice. I messed up in school from 2nd all the way up to 5th grade, and it got my parents really mad at me. They explained that talking and fooling around in class are not the way school works. That discussion helped start my 180-degree turnaround in school. They made me see that life doesn't mean anything if you fail. It didn't happen overnight, but I gradually started to take that step in the right direction.

My father has always tried to keep us from making the same mistakes he made as a child. One mistake I think he made was not going to college. He was smart enough to do anything, but no one encouraged him to do it. His parents discouraged him from fulfilling a dream, so I think that is why he encourages us to do well in school.

"I never had anyone behind me like we're behind you, Stephen," my parents often tell me. My father wants me to move on to better things in life. No one in the family has gone to college yet. My father isn't just tough, though. He also loves to hug and kiss, which can be embarrassing. He's also very playful, and it doesn't take much to get him started.

He is very open, so you can often find us sitting down and talking. He tells me about when he was my age, about life, and a good joke every now and then. I talk to him (and my mother) about all my problems, my achievements, and my life.

One point my father stresses with me and my friends is being a man. Nowadays, when boys think being a man is having a baby or having sex with lots of girls, he tells us that a real man would care for the baby he made and doesn't need to "hit anything in a skirt." Sometimes me and my boys will act too macho (sometimes if we see a girl, we start hooting, hollering, and flexing our muscles), but he'll pull us aside and tell us it doesn't take all that.

My father gives good advice. And I love that he will always tell me, my brother, sister, and my mother that he loves us. He says it any time, when we're playing around, before he leaves for work, or when something "big" happens to us. Usually things like that only happen on TV, but he'll pause and tell us, "just so we'll know."

Stephen was 17 when he wrote this story.
He graduated from Mercy College.

Kaite Martin

In an Octopus's Garden

By Dina Spanbock

"I'd like to be under the sea in an octopus's garden in the shade." I was in the living room with my dad, listening to his original vinyl Beatles record playing the song "Octopus's Garden." I was about 6 years old, and that line troubled me. It wasn't the idea of a person being under the sea and hanging out with an octopus that bothered me. The issue I had was with the shade.

"How can there be shade under the sea?" I asked my dad. "There aren't shady spots and sunny spots under water!"

My father told me that it was make-believe, so it didn't need to make sense. That opened up my eyes. Music and other types of art didn't need to be realistic all the time. I embraced the idea of creativity, and I was drawn to the arts, especially music.

Music has always been a huge part of my life. I attribute

that mostly to my father, who passed away three years ago. He loved music, and he instilled that love in me. We bonded through music, and I continue to connect to him through it.

Some of my earliest memories involve my father and music. We always listened together to the radio, CDs, and his vinyl records. He chose the music, mostly classic rock, but sometimes he'd play classical music or smooth jazz when I couldn't sleep.

As I grew older, I began to follow in the footsteps of my older sister and peers, listening to popular music of the day, like Christina Aguilera and *NSYNC.

I realized that my father and I were both individuals with our own pasts and interests.

But as I neared the end of middle school, something made me go back to my dad's music. I don't remember why, but one day I wanted to listen to the Ramones, a pop-punk band from the '70s and '80s. I went to my father's CD collection and found a solo album by Joey Ramone, the lead singer, from after the band broke up.

As I lay in bed listening to the bright pink CD, I thought about my father and the connection he must have to the music. He could remember when the Ramones were popular, when they broke up, when these albums had come out. They were a part of his life outside of mine.

It made me realize that he wasn't just my father, but a person who had his own life and everything that came along with it, including a childhood. We were both individuals with our own pasts and interests. We had this connection as people now, not just as father and daughter.

A few months later, soon after I began high school, my friend and I were walking in New York City's Central Park late one afternoon when I heard what sounded like guitars. We followed the sound and found ourselves surrounded by a group of people singing and playing Beatles songs.

It turned out it was John Lennon's 64th birthday. (One of the lead members of the Beatles, Lennon was killed in 1980.) That was a significant anniversary because of The Beatles' song "When I'm 64." Fans had come to pay tribute to Lennon in Strawberry Fields, the area of Central Park dedicated to him. I thought the chords, rhythms, harmonies, and lyrics were beautiful.

I went home that night and headed to my dad's CD collection again, this time looking for Beatles albums. I listened to them repeatedly for the next few weeks, learning all the songs.

Because of my dad, music isn't just a pastime for me. It's a passion and a reason to live.

One evening, I sat down at the computer in my dad's bedroom to do my homework. I put on The Beatles' *Rubber Soul* album and sang along to the first song, "Drive My Car." By the time the second track, "Norwegian Wood (This Bird Has Flown)," began, my dad had walked into the room and was standing near me, singing along as he often did.

We smiled and looked at each other as we sang harmonies and drummed our hands on our thighs with the beat. We didn't speak because we didn't have to. The music spoke for us.

Meanwhile, a new source of music had come into my life. I began to take voice lessons when I was 13. My voice teacher introduced me to songs from musicals, something my dad didn't listen to often. My first performance was a school talent show, only months after I began voice lessons.

I walked on stage, so shaky I was afraid I'd fall over in my high heels. I breathed deeply and prepared for that first note as I brought the microphone up to my mouth. "I hope you never lose your sense of wonder," I sang (from the song "I Hope You Dance," by Lee Ann Womack). Before I knew it, the song was over.

I walked off the stage in a daze from the rush of performing in front of a large audience. When I found my father, he was beaming with pride. He'd heard me sing around the house, but this was the first time he'd heard me giving it my all the way I do in voice lessons and performances. We hugged and he told me how lucky he felt to be my father. For weeks afterwards he proudly told me about all the people who had complimented my performance to him.

Looking back, I think my singing deepened our musical relationship. Before, he would offer bands, songs, and music-related facts, and I would receive them. It was my interest in a passion of his. Now I was sharing my own musical passion with him. I was giving something back to him: my voice, my musical creations.

My father passed away suddenly when I was 15 years old, not long after I rediscovered the Beatles. A few months later, I had a performance in a concert my voice teacher was organizing. I decided to sing "Papa Can You Hear Me," a song that the main character in the musical *Yentl* sings to her father after he passes away.

I, too, sang the song for my father. I had a very bittersweet feeling on stage. It was extremely emotional—difficult because my father wasn't with me physically, but also incredibly fulfilling to be doing something I loved that he'd inspired me to do and that I know he would have wanted me to pursue.

After the performance, lots of people came and complimented me. One woman I didn't know said she could tell that I had lost a loved one. She told me I sang the song with the emotion that only someone who intimately knew loss could have. I told her that my father had passed away earlier that year and that he had inspired my passion for music and singing.

Listening to and singing music has helped me cope with my father's death because of all the happiness it brings me, and because I know that he would be happy to see me continuing this love. He may not be with me physically, but as long as there is music, he will always be with me spiritually.

To this day, I always privately dedicate my performances to my father. And I always listen to music with him in mind. It is because of him that I love music, and his genetics gave me my musical ear. Because of him, music isn't just a pastime for me. It is a passion, a reason to live, something that never fails to make me happy.

Dina was 18 when she wrote this story.
She later attended Hampshire College.

Gary Smith

Hurting Myself for His Attention

By Natalie Olivero

By the time I was 4 years old, my father didn't live with us anymore. He'd come to see my younger sister and me at our apartment, but not very often and he wouldn't stay long. I remember Daddy promising to come see us one summer day when I was 5. When I woke up that morning, I asked my mother, "Is Daddy coming today?" I wanted to be sure.

"Your father should be on his way," she said.

My sister and I ate breakfast and the time kept ticking by. After another few hours, we were eating our lunch and there was still no sign of him. After another couple of hours, I asked my mother again when he was coming. She didn't know.

The day was almost over when my father called to say he'd run into some trouble and couldn't make it. "Why do you always tell them that you're coming and never show up?" my mother asked. As usual he didn't have an answer, and they got into a fight. I felt sad because I couldn't understand why my father wouldn't come to see me.

I've always wanted Daddy be a real father, to love me and pay attention to me. But I've never been able to get him to visit me regularly or come to graduations, award ceremonies, or other important events in my life.

My mother said Daddy left when I was little because he couldn't stand my grandmother (my mom's mom) living with us. Maybe that was partially true, but I think he wanted to be with another woman. He often doesn't tell the truth.

Even though he didn't live with us, I still wanted to have the father-daughter relationship other girls in my school had with their dads. I wanted him to come to parent-teacher nights at my school so he could see my good grades. I wanted to talk to him about things my mother didn't know about, like cars, repairing things, and other guy stuff.

Instead, Daddy would drop in and out of my life, sometimes appearing without warning and then not reappearing for years at a time. In 5th grade, he showed up on picture day at my elementary school. I hadn't seen him in two years.

At that moment, I was so happy to see him that I didn't care how long he'd been away. I remember I was wearing a flowered dress, boots and a hat with a flower on it. My father asked my mother, "Why does she look like a cowgirl?" That made my mother, my sister, and me laugh.

But those good times were rare. When I was about to graduate from elementary school, I had a dream that both of my parents were in the audience watching me get my diploma, and Daddy was so proud of me. I woke up crying because I knew he wouldn't show up in real life. And he didn't.

Sometimes I hate my father for leaving us. My mother was diagnosed with epilepsy when she was 11, and she suffers from seizures. I've always had to take care of her and my younger sister, and a lot of times the pressure has been too much for me. I get so scared when my mother has a seizure. If it wasn't for my grandmother being around, I think I'd have gone completely crazy by now.

By 9th grade, my first year of high school, I felt so hurt by my dad abandoning me that I started to act out. I was cutting classes and coming home late. I chilled from 7 in the morning till 2 the next morning, hanging with my friends on their block.

I wanted to see if my father would pay attention to me if I continued to misbehave.

With more than 2,000 students in the school, no guidance counselor or teacher noticed my absences for a year. It wasn't until fall of my sophomore year that my mom found out I was cutting, when a school official finally called her. My mother called my father, which was what I secretly wanted her to do.

I figured cutting was the best way to make him pay attention to me, and I was right. He started coming to our apartment to tell me that I should go to school because "it's important to have an education." I ignored him. Why did he think I'd take advice from a man who didn't care about me enough to show up when I was little?

One day during summer school, my mother told me my father was waiting downstairs. He had just moved upstate, but he had come back down to New York City to see me. When I got downstairs to take the train to school, he told me to get into his car.

"Are you going to take me to school now?" I asked.

"No, you're coming with me, so call your boyfriend and let him know that you're not going to see him today," he said. "You're going to stay with me all day."

That didn't make any sense! Why would he force me to go with him, only to refuse to take me to school? Maybe he blamed my boyfriend for my cutting (which wasn't true) and wanted to keep us apart. Then the day got even more confusing. My father's girlfriend had decided to visit a relative's house upstate, and he made me go with them. When we reached the house, my father started hanging out and drinking. I sat around bored, watching everyone else have fun. By midnight, he was still drinking when I asked him to take me home.

"Are you crazy? I can't drive drunk," he said, handing me his phone so I could call my mother to say I wasn't coming home. When he finally drove me home the next day, I still didn't go to school. I wanted to see if my father would pay attention to me if I continued to misbehave.

At first, it worked. He continued to take me upstate with him, and keep me for days or weeks at a time without sending me to school. But after three months of that, I think he must have gotten tired of it, because he stopped showing up at my house. When my mother called him for help, he didn't answer his phone anymore.

After three years of cutting, I finally realized that I wasn't going to get what I needed from him by not going to school. There was no magic moment, no profound conversation with my mother or my best friend that made me see the light. One morning I just woke up and realized I was only hurting myself by cutting school.

I felt bad because my friends were telling me that they were passing when I wasn't. Then a couple of friends transferred to other schools, and they told me they were doing better. I was missing too many credits to graduate so I decided to transfer to a new school, too.

I told my mother that I was going to change and take school seriously if she helped get me into a new school. So she put me on the waiting list for an alternative school. Now I'm in my third year there and I'm loving it. I'm developing my passion for reading and writing. With only 200 students in the entire school, my teachers give me more attention than I ever got at my last school.

And I don't cut anymore because I want to graduate in January and go to college.

My father hasn't contacted me in five months, and he doesn't call me back when I call him. I'm trying to not hurt myself anymore just because my father has hurt me. I love him but I feel like I'm the only one loving without getting anything back in return.

I'm going to keep my heart open in case he wants to open his heart to me.

But I haven't given up on him. When I'm ready to start my own family, I'm going to call my father and give him the chance to try erase all the bad memories I have about him. I'm going to keep my heart open in case he wants to open his heart to me.

When I do call my father, I hope he'll want to pick me up and hang out with me. Or I can just hop on the railroad and go upstate to see him. That way he can't say he's too busy to hang out with me. But I know that eventually I'll have to give up. When I have children of my own, I don't want him to make promises to them that he'll never keep.

Natalie was 18 when she wrote this story.

David Najarro

Not My Idea of a Father

By Anonymous

Some of my earliest memories of my father involve his old car, a Ford Maverick. I loved that car, the way it looked and the way it smelled. It was white with a light brown roof and silver trim. It had this wonderful smell I looked forward to inhaling every time we went for a ride. I usually didn't know where we were going, and I didn't care. I was stuck in the house a lot so those drives were a treat for me, even if we didn't go anywhere special.

I remember other good things about my relationship with my father back then. When I was about 6, we had a bedtime ritual. Every night at 10 p.m. we would go into the bedroom, usually by ourselves, and he would take our puzzles out of the drawer. He would do the crossword puzzles and I would do the circle-the-word puzzles until I fell asleep.

My father was also the one that got me into cartoons. We

would sit in front of the TV, laughing, howling, and crying as we watched Woody Woodpecker or Bugs Bunny. I still remember the way my dad laughed, a very loud "AH HA HA HA." I remember him as being very happy and jolly, joking around a lot.

I also remember some bad times, like when my parents fought. I don't remember what their arguments were about, but I remember feeling like the world was ending whenever they had one. My mother would be yelling and screaming, with tears running down her face. Her voice made this kind of shrill sound when she screamed. I thought she was physically hurt. I would sit in a closet screaming and crying, "What's wrong with my Mommy?" My older sister would comfort me until my mother came to show me she was all right.

I was about 7 when my dad moved out. I don't remember anyone telling me he was leaving. I didn't even notice at first that he was gone, strange as it may

I wanted my dad to tell me about his life and give me advice.

sound. I was probably used to him not being around because he used to disappear for weeks at a time before he left for good.

After that, he would still come by every once in a while to take me and my brothers to the movies. I didn't miss him when he was gone, but when he did show up, I was usually excited. It meant we were going somewhere. He took us to McDonald's, White Castle, the movies, the park, to visit relatives, and for rides in the car.

My father and I hung out together but we never really talked, not about significant things anyway. Sure I told him about school, my report card, and what I wanted for Christmas, but that's about it. I felt that there was something missing from our relationship, that there should have been more of a father-son bond. I wanted him to tell me about where he came from, tell me about his life, give me advice. But maybe he thought I wasn't old enough for those kinds of discussions.

Dealing With Dad

Although my mother never tried to stop me from seeing my father, I knew she wasn't happy about it. She would frequently sit me down and tell me he wasn't doing his job as a parent. Whenever I came home from seeing him, she would take me alone in a room and grill me about where we went and what we did together. Maybe she wanted to make sure I wasn't being mistreated. Or maybe she resented me wanting to see him at all.

I knew she wasn't angry at me; she just disliked my father. But I felt I indirectly and unfairly caught her wrath and I resented it. I felt like she didn't trust my judgment. It seemed like she expected me to run off and live with my father, like I couldn't figure out for myself that she was doing a better job as a parent.

The truth is, I didn't know how I felt about my father. He used to say he loved me a lot when I was out with him, but I don't remember my responses. I do know it was different from when my mom said she loved me. I don't know why, I just think I understood how much she cared without even needing to be told.

On my 14th birthday my father took me to see *Batman*. The whole thing was a big adventure for me—going out at night in a neighborhood I had never been to before. We came in at the middle of the movie so he agreed to let me watch it again. Afterwards, my father dropped me off at home and that was the last time I saw him for four years. There was no warning; he just didn't come around any more after that.

My father dropped me off at home and that was the last time I saw him for four years.

For two years I carried the ticket stubs from that movie in my wallet. (My father always used to give me the stubs when we went to the movies.) Then, one night when I was 16, I took out my wallet and looked at those stubs. Tears welled up in my eyes as I thought about that night at the movies. I walked to the bathroom with tears streaming down my face. I ripped up the stubs and flushed them down the toilet.

I decided that I had no father. How could I call that man "Dad" when he was never around and I knew nothing about him? I didn't know what kind of person he was or what kind of personality he had. I wasn't even sure of his birth date.

Maybe he did care. Maybe he did love me. But when you say you love someone you have to prove it, you have to show it. My definition of a father is someone who is always going to be there for his child. As the saying goes, "Any fool can make a baby, but it takes a man to raise one." A father makes sacrifices, he cares and worries until it hurts, and beyond. He is understanding and fair. He takes the time to know his child. As far as I could see, my father hadn't done most of those things.

Then last summer, two years after I had ripped up those ticket stubs, he showed up at my house. I wasn't there, but the rest of the family was. They told me afterwards how old he looked, with a sprinkling of gray hairs and a dark, haggard face. They told me he stared in disbelief when he saw how big my brothers had gotten.

They showed him a picture of me. Squinting his eyes, he looked at it and asked, "That's Scott?" I tried to imagine him saying that and looking at my picture. What did he look like? How did he sound?

I just couldn't believe it. After four years my father came back and I missed it! He had left a number where I could contact him but I didn't run to the phone. For one thing, I was scared. I didn't know how I would feel seeing him again.

I was also worried about how my mother would react. For years I had to sit down and listen to her go on about the job my father didn't do. She never had anything good to say about him. What would she say if I told her I wanted to get in touch with my father again? That I wanted to find out what kind of person he is? I was sure she would say, "Why would you want to see him? He's just no good and all he's going to bring is trouble."

I thought about all of that for two or three weeks and finally decided to make the call and set up a meeting. A couple of days later, one of my brothers came over to me while I was watching TV and told me my father was at the door.

He was in uniform because he drove a bus. He was a couple of inches shorter than me. I saw the specks of gray in his hair. His face looked weathered and greasy. He had a small beer belly. His West Indian accent was so thick I couldn't believe that we were related—I don't have a trace of an accent. I shook his hand and we greeted each other.

We went outside and sat down to talk. I studied every inch of him. I kept looking at his face so I wouldn't forget what he looked like. I have photo albums with pictures of him, but it hurts to look at them. I tried to talk to him about my memories. I told him I was shocked that he had an accent. "Yeah, I have an accent," he said without emotion.

He started to go into why he left. He said it was because of his troubles with my mother and didn't have anything to do with his children. He asked why I hadn't tried to get in touch with him.

He said he left because of his troubles with my mother; it had nothing to do with his children.

It was a subtle guilt trip, but I paid no attention. I was more interested in getting to know him.

But when he mentioned it a second time, I got angry. "I don't have to call you week after week, what do you think this is?!" Maybe he felt I was obligated to call him because he's my father. Or maybe he wanted to blame someone else for the fact that he's lost his sons. But whose fault is it that he hadn't come to see us in four years?

My father and I still see each other from time to time, and things remain tense between us. I am finding out bits and pieces about his past, which is my past as well. I still want to get to know him but, at the same time, I don't want to give him the satisfaction of being able to call me "son" and act like a proud father when I feel he hasn't earned it. I also still wonder if my spending time with him is hurting my mother. I want to do the right thing, but I don't know what the right thing is. It seems like no matter what I do someone is going to get hurt—my mother, my father, or me.

The author was 18 when he wrote this story. He later graduated from college and worked in financial.

Karolina Zaniesienko

Understanding Father's Love

By Chun Lar Tom

Growing up in China, I often felt sad when I saw Father sitting home alone. I wanted to talk to him. But I didn't, because even though we were living in the same house, my father was a stranger to me. I feared him. And I didn't know if he loved me.

Father was strong and dark-skinned because he worked under the sun. He harvested crops, watered fields, and cut weeds. He hardly smiled.

When I saw Father, I always said "Baba," which means "Father." That's considered respectful and polite in my culture. He nodded and then I went away as quickly as I could.

I thought he was too strict and old-fashioned. Sometimes, when I was excited and talked loudly, he told me to lower my voice because he thought good girls were supposed to talk quietly. And I had to go to bed by 9 every night, even after I turned 12.

Father was quiet and usually didn't try to talk to me, except to say, "How's school?"

"Good," I'd reply.

I always gave him short answers because I didn't feel comfortable talking to him. "You have to study hard so you can have a good future," he told me. "Look at your cousins. They all have good grades in school. Everybody in the village knows that and praises them. Don't be the stupid one in the family."

I sometimes wondered if Father loved me less because I was a girl.

I hated when Father compared me to my cousins, because he made me feel like I was a product at the market. Still, I pushed myself to get good grades in school because I thought if I could please him, he'd care for me more.

I sometimes wondered if Father loved me less because I was a girl. In China, many people prefer boys. Since I was little, I'd heard people in my village gossiping about how my father wanted a boy. He'd ended up with me and my two younger sisters, Bik Bik and Pui Pui.

Thankfully, my mother made me feel like she cared for me a lot. She cooked dishes that she knew I liked and asked me questions about how I felt, which Father never did. I talked to her about my friends and dreams. I never told Mom how I felt toward Father, but I think she knew.

As I got older, I still wasn't sure where my fear of Father came from. Was it from the seriousness of his face? Or the lack of communication between us? Or my uncertainty about his love for me? This fear followed me like a shadow until one unforgettable day when I was 14.

That morning, Father asked me to go to market with him. I'd had a stomachache for a few days, but I didn't want to disappoint him. So I went. Vendors from different villages came to our village to sell everything from pork to bamboo baskets. The streets were so crowded that we moved as slowly as turtles.

We stopped in front of a skinny woman selling fruit. As Father asked her the price of her apples, I felt my stomach hurt. I put my hands on my stomach and squeezed hard, trying to stop the pain because I didn't want to worry Father.

Father paid for the apples, put them in his basket and walked forward. I walked slowly behind him, fighting with the pain. I felt like thousands of wriggling worms were eating the inside of my stomach. I fell far behind as the pain grew bigger and bigger. But my father didn't turn around.

"Baba! Baba, wait! Wait for me!" I shouted. But my words were swallowed by the noise.

I sat down on the street. Sweat streamed down my face. Tears started to fill my eyes. Father appeared in front of me, angry. "What are you doing here?" he said. But the anger in his eyes changed immediately into worry when he saw my face.

"Are you OK?" he asked.

"My stomach hurts," I said. I started to cry.

"I'll get you to the hospital," he said.

Father threw the basket away and held my arms around his neck. "Hold tight," he said, and started running. He kept yelling, "Excuse me! Excuse me!" trying to get through the crowd. Sweat from his face dropped on my hands like rain, followed by his urgent breaths.

It usually took us 30 minutes to get to the hospital. We made it in 15. "Doctor, doctor, please help my daughter," Father yelled as he grabbed the shirt of the first doctor he saw. The doctor asked him what happened, then gave me a shot as Father held my hands and whispered into my ear, "You're going to be fine." Then I fell asleep.

It turned out I had a worm in my intestine, causing the terrible pain. The doctor gave me a few more shots to kill the worm. I had to stay in the hospital for one night. Father was afraid that the worm was still alive. He asked the doctor how to handle it in case my stomach hurt again. He kept shaking the doctor's hand, saying, "Thank you, doctor. Thank you so much."

I was shocked by his behavior. I didn't realize how much he cared for me. When I got home from the hospital, Father wanted me to stay home from school and rest for a few days.

"I have a test soon," I said.

"Don't worry. You'll be fine," Father said.

"Don't worry? Don't worry? You'd better not say anything if I fail the test," I said.

I pretended I was asleep when he came to my room at dinnertime. Father didn't say anything. After he left, I saw my favorite noodles were in a big bowl on the desk. White steam spiraled up gently from the bowl. I knew it was Father who cooked them because only he cooked such tasty noodles. Suddenly, a warm feeling filled my heart. Looking at the noodles, my mind focused on how Father

Father must've gotten up late at night and cooked the noodles for me under the dim light in the kitchen.

must've gotten up late at night and cooked them under the dim light in the kitchen. I felt embraced by his love.

Since that time, our relationship has slowly changed. During the first few months after my illness, I began to talk to Father more because I wanted to understand him. I knew now that he loved me, so I felt more comfortable reaching out to him, which made him open up.

Father was still generally quiet, but sometimes told me stories from his past, like when he thought he was grabbing a fish from a river and discovered it was a snake. My heart ached when I heard how he was beaten up during China's Cultural Revolution, a period of government repression. As Father shared more, I felt comfortable telling him about my friends and school. We came to America when I was 15, and since then, we've become closer.

Sometimes he still compares me to my cousins, but not as much as before. I know he doesn't mean to hurt me. I tell myself that he uses my cousins as examples to encourage me to study hard.

Once, when I was 16, Father told me, "I know you think I'm too strict, but I push you hard because I want you to have a better life. The better education you have, the better chance you'll have a good job in the future. I am doing this not for myself, but for you." I began to realize that Father was strict because he cared about me so much.

Mom's happy that our relationship has changed as well. "Now I wouldn't be surprised to see you and your father sit down and talk for an hour," she said.

Just before we came to America, my parents had a baby boy, Hong. Father treats Hong the way he treated me and my sisters when we were little. So I realized that Father didn't treat me differently because I was a girl.

Now I know that the seriousness of his face masks a heart filled with love for me. I often fondly remember how Father took care of me when I was sick because that's the first time I was able to see his love. Still, I've never told him how I once feared him greatly or how I feel about him now. I don't know why, because I really want to tell him, "Baba, I love you."

Chun Lar was 18 when she wrote this story.
After high school, she went to Bard College.

David Najarro

Not My Father's Daughter

By Sarvenaz Ezzati

In July I got a letter in an airmail envelope with Islamic stamps and Farsi writing on it. I immediately recognized that it was from Iran, the country I fled with my mother nine years ago, when I was 8. The sender was my father, Kourosh Ezzati. Even though I haven't seen him in more than seven years, I'm still afraid of him.

I've always felt that if my father wanted to he could take me back to Iran. And since a girl belongs to her father like property there, he would have the right to marry me off to someone of his choice and get a dowry in exchange. Many times he threatened my mother that he would kidnap me and take me back to Iran. This caused me to be very wary of all Iranians, because I know how persuasive my father can be. If he said the right words, he could get anyone to help him.

Since my mother and I felt any Iranian we met could have

been a spy for my father, we avoided contact with other Iranians, even family friends. When we first came to this country and socialized with other Iranian families, adults would casually ask me questions about my mother and myself, and then convey the information back to my father. We soon learned to avoid other Iranians—especially Iranian men.

Then one day last summer, I heard two Iranian men on the train speaking Farsi, fluently and eloquently. I became very emotional and depressed. I realized how much of my Iranian culture and heritage I had given up because I was trying to protect myself from my father. I will probably never again dance the special Persian dances I once loved. Or attend festive parties like the ones I remember going to with my parents in Iran, where all generations celebrated together, guests were treated like royalty, and everyone shared huge plates of delicious meat stews and rice. For a moment, these happy memories allowed me to forget the dark side of thoughts about my father and my country.

Many times my father threatened to kidnap me and take me back to Iran.

Iran is now a place I fear and would never go back to voluntarily. It's a very religious and old-fashioned country. Women are supposed to be passive and quiet, and they are considered the weaker sex, mentally and physically. When the Ayatollah Khomeini seized power in 1979, overthrowing the Shah of Iran, he wanted to lead the country with the laws of the Koran, the Islamic holy book.

Through his own personal translations of the Islamic laws, Khomeini took the rights of women away, forcing them again to wear black chadors (a veil that covers the entire body), denying them educational opportunities (the majority of Iranian women were illiterate), and telling Iranian men that knowledge for a woman was dangerous because women are not capable of working and making decisions for themselves.

The radical change from the Shah, who was very modern

in his ideas about women's roles, to the repressive Ayatollah Khomeini literally happened overnight. One morning my mother woke up and realized she was the property of my father and that all her rights had been taken away. She also knew that any educational opportunities I would have had under the Shah were now nonexistent. We were like free birds suddenly trapped in a cage of religious oppression and darkness.

As the country became more oppressive, my mother's life there became unbearable. My mother speaks five different languages, was a straight-A student in high school, and upon graduation at the age of 18, began teaching Air Force pilots how to speak, read, and write English. But she never went to college because her father felt she should be married and that college for a girl was a waste of money.

When my mother married my father, she loved him and looked forward to a happily-ever-after relationship despite warning signals, like the other girlfriends he flaunted. It wasn't long after they were married that my father started to lie to my mother, and sleep around. When he was angry, he beat her.

My father's approach to running his business was no better than his approach to marriage. Eventually, dishonest business dealings landed him in jail. Since my mother had helped out in his business, she knew the authorities were preparing to come after her, too. This hastened her decision to flee the country.

Here in the U.S., I've been raised to think of myself as equal to men and to make decisions for myself. I fear going back to Iran because I would not be able to go to college, have a career of my own, or even wear what clothing I like. I know that I could never live like the many Iranian women who take orders from their husbands and are financially and socially dependent. If a woman is not married in Iran, or if she is divorced, she is considered rotten, like spoiled milk. I could never survive in such an oppressive environment.

Young women in this country take for granted that they can

go to college, dress how they please, and choose for themselves who they will marry. I, on the other hand, am always afraid that I will lose my opportunities to get an education and start my own career. I fear that I will end up married to a man like my father.

When I received my father's letter, my feelings of fear mixed with distrust. Because of the person he is, I know that even a letter that says nice things may contain danger.

My mother and I left Iran after struggling for four years to get green cards. My father promised to join us in the United States once he took care of his business. (Even after everything he did to her, my mother was willing to give him another chance.) But after three years he told my mother that he wanted us to return to Iran instead.

His reason was that he didn't want to give up his $1 million business in Iran. He told us that the situation for women in Iran had improved. But he was lying—Iranian women still had no rights. It didn't seem to bother him that in Iran I wouldn't be able to go to college or have a career. He just didn't want to give up his business. I felt abandoned because his money meant more to him than I did.

I wasn't really surprised to get a letter from my father because occasionally he sends me something saying that he still thinks about me. He sometimes sends me gifts from Iran, telling me he cares for me, and that any unhappiness I feel is because of my mother. His gifts always feel like bribes to turn me against my mother. Instead, my trust in him lessens with every gift.

But there was something in this letter that I never expected. My father said that it was his duty as a father to pay for my college education—a bill my mother can't pay alone.

Now I feel that I'm being bribed once again, but the stakes are higher. He's willing to pay for my entire college education. This could be the chance of a lifetime. Since my grades are average, it's not very likely that I can get a full scholarship or grant. And it would be a big luxury if I could graduate college without a loan to pay back afterwards. With the money my mother would save, she could afford to send me abroad to study in London or Paris, and give me extra spending money.

Yet I feel like I'm being bought, and that if I accept the offer I would be letting my father off the hook. For the price of my college education, my father would want forgiveness and a second chance to be the father he never was.

My father said that it was his duty to pay for my college education. I feel that I'm being bribed.

I have to make my decision soon and it isn't an easy one, not like winning Lotto, where someone hands me a big fat check with no strings attached. After all, why would he make this offer without expecting me to allow him into my life again? If he pays, he could expect me to play the role of dutiful daughter. And, if I accept, I'll be committed to a relationship with him that I might not be ready for.

Sarvenaz was 17 when she wrote this story. She graduated from high school and college and became a school teacher.

Gary Smith

Discovering My Dad
at the Movies

By Daniela Castillo

One day when I was 8 years old, I decided to snoop through my dad's bedroom closet. Inside I found a giant faded leather trunk, which I imagined was filled with precious jewels or other treasure.

Knowing that Dad was busy on his computer in the living room, I pulled the trunk out and opened it. Instead of finding treasure, I saw stacks of old magazines called *Rolling Stone*, which I'd never heard of. I assumed it was porn, which I'd recently learned about from my cousins. Not only was my dad a man who didn't talk to me—he was a pervert too! The idea that my dad looked at the things my older cousins talked about so feverishly made me feel weird.

At first, I didn't want to have anything more to do with my

dad. He was quiet and withdrawn, so I didn't feel much of a connection to him anyway. But then I began to feel sorry for him because he read porn magazines and saved them in his closet. I still liked him, so I decided not to give up on him yet.

My parents divorced when I was 3 and I'd lived with my mom ever since. I visited my dad at his house 10 minutes away, but we didn't have conversations when I was there.

I wanted a playful and loving relationship like my friend Imani had with her dad. But my dad was not one to chat. He needed to be explaining something or really interested to get excited about anything. When he talked to his friends about movies or things they did together, I'd see him acting very enthusiastic and animated. But when I was around, he'd only talk about the news or his job.

One thing I knew Dad really liked was movies—he had a whole wall in his house devoted to them, with names like *M* and *8 1/2*. I never bothered to ask him about his movie obsession because I figured he'd tell me if he wanted me to share his hobbies.

But the porn bothered me. So that night during dinner, I decided to confront him. "What are those, uh, magazines in your closet?"

"What, my *Rolling Stones*?" he said.

The nerve of him! To admit it, like everybody had a trunk full of decomposing porn magazines in their closet. "They're my magazines from when I was 14 or so," he said.

My fears began to fade. I knew my grandmother wouldn't have let my father have porn magazines. Dad explained that *Rolling Stone* was dedicated to music and movies, and that the magazine was still being published. He said I was too young to understand what was in the magazines but that he'd let me read them one day. He had a glow the rest of the night, like he had something up his sleeve.

As he was driving me back to my mom's house the next

morning, he asked, "So, why were you looking through my closet?" I told him I was bored.

"Next time you come over, we'll do something fun," he said.

For the rest of the week, I couldn't wait to see what my dad was planning. I imagined getting a pet, maybe a rare breed of monkey. When he picked me up, he said we were going to a museum. I was so delusional that I thought maybe we were going to the museum to get the weird monkey!

When we pulled up to the Museum of the Moving Image, I could see there wasn't going to be any monkey inside that building. I felt too disappointed to protest. If this was the best he could do, I had to accept that my dad was dull and only concerned with his own interests.

I wanted a playful and loving relationship. But my dad was not one to chat.

But I was wrong. Once we got inside, Dad took me to see a series of optical illusions, sculptures, and lighting displays that I could have stared at forever. After about 15 minutes, he convinced me that there were even cooler things to see. We saw displays with actual movie sets and props, including a Chucky doll used in one of the *Chucky* horror movies (about a doll that kills people). And we made flipbooks of Dad and me sticking our tongues out and acting like monkeys.

After we left the museum, I wondered why it took me rummaging through his closet for him to do something so fun with me. But I already knew the answer: My dad is shy and I had to bring him out of his shell to have fun. From that day forward, I asked my dad to take me to the movies. I wondered if he'd think I was dumb for liking animated movies like *A Bug's Life* and *Shrek* instead of the fancy French movies he watched. But every time I laughed, he laughed, and I knew he was happy that I was having fun.

By the time I was 12, Dad was taking me to some of his favorite movies. Once we went to a screening of *Rashomon* at an arthouse theater in Manhattan called the Film Forum. He told me it was a very special place to him and that he'd been coming here for years. Dad rarely told me about things that were important to him, so it gave the occasion a sense of discovery.

When we got there, I thought the place looked too small for a movie theater. I was used to the big multi-level theaters with giant screens. The Film Forum had only 15 rows of chairs with about 20 seats in each row.

The few people who were there looked like older versions of my dad: weird old bearded men wearing corduroy suits, college professors, and cleaned-up homeless-looking people. It sure wasn't the museum, and I was worried my dad was reverting to his old boring ways.

Rashomon turned out to be a black and white Japanese movie about four people giving different accounts of a rape and murder. Now it's one of my favorite movies, but when I saw it for the first time, I didn't understand that it was about people distorting reality.

Why had my dad taken me to see it? I hated that I still had to pry everything out of him. Maybe he expected me to understand the movie. Maybe he didn't know how to be a parent. I was aggravated about having to work so hard to figure out my dad.

But that didn't stop me from asking him questions. As we were getting into his car, I asked him why he liked *Rashomon* so much. Dad said it was beautiful to watch and the acting was so great and subtle.

I had never heard him speak so passionately about anything before. I'd always seen him as an anti-social person who didn't like to talk, but now I saw him as a man with feelings, who liked things because he sympathized with them. After *Rashomon*, I liked my dad as a father and an intellectual. He'd always find interesting facts to tell me about the movies we went to see, and soon I wanted to know everything there was to know about directors, actors, and critics.

I found *New Yorker* magazine movie critic Pauline Kael on the Internet, and I liked her reviews. When I asked my dad if he knew her work, he said, "Of course!" and gave me several of her books to read.

I loved Kael's critiques because she treated movies as if they were breathing, living, walking beings, and she wrote as if she liked, despised, or loved each particular being. I went on a mission to see every movie she'd reviewed, and so far I've seen about 200. (I'm a little obsessed with movies now, just like my dad.)

I'd watch the movies and re-read her reviews and, every time, she brought up a new point of view or small detail that I had missed. Man, this Kael lady was a genius! By the time I turned 14, I'd decided that I wanted to become a film journalist and write just as passionately and creatively as Pauline Kael. I've started journalism classes at my school this year and I hope to write for my school newspaper.

Before we started going to the movies together, loving my dad felt like an obligation.

And it's all thanks to my dad. Before we started going to the movies together, loving my dad felt like an obligation, not something I felt because we had a great relationship. Movies showed us how similar our tastes are (our favorite director is François Truffaut and we love French movies). Even when we don't agree, our discussions bring us closer. We love to debate what's the best movie we've seen during the year. He'll usually win, but I can never get mad at him because his arguments are usually pretty good.

Watching movies together also made me realize that my dad is a cool guy. Last Halloween he was going out with some friends and dressed up like the character David St. Hubbins from the movie, *This Is Spinal Tap*. And he can recite the whole script from the movie, *Monty Python and the Holy Grail*. His humor is alot like mine—spontaneous and offbeat.

Having my dad introduce me to the world of movies was better than any trip to the park with him. And knowing that my dad and I can have conversations about things that we both feel so strongly about gives me a sense of family that wasn't complete before. I have great relationships with all of my family members, but the most important one—with my father—wasn't there until we got to know each other at the movie theater.

Daniela was 14 when she wrote this story.
She later attended college, majoring in film.

Steven Mattor

The Guy I Call My Dad

By Anonymous

The guy I call dad has been the thorn of my life. He is imposing. He is selfish. He resents me, because he can no longer control me, and I resent him for the pain he's caused me and my family.

My father lashes out at people when he can't get his way. My mother has suffered most because of this. When I was little, he'd hit her, like every couple of months. Once, when we were waiting for the train, he got upset that it was taking so long. So my mom told him, "Calm down. It's gonna come when it's gonna come."

Some ladies overheard this and began to laugh a little. My father stormed off, saying he was going to take a cab home. After they got home, my mother and father started arguing. He felt like he was the butt of a joke, that the ladies were laughing at him and that my mom embarrassed him. My mother kept arguing because she likes to have the last word. I was in another room, but I could

70

hear everything. The arguing got worse until I heard furniture banging against the wall, like two people were wrestling.

I was usually in another room when my father hit my mom. The few times I saw her getting hit, I can't remember too well. My mom never had bruises, but I always heard crashes and her crying, which made me know he was hitting her.

When I heard my mom getting hit, I tried to act normal, but I was really scared and my adrenaline would be running so fast. I prayed to myself, hoping it would end and that he would just leave her alone. Afterwards, I usually asked her if she was OK. I'd ask if could do anything to help, and she'd say no. Then we all made believe it didn't happen.

Thankfully, my pops hardly ever hit me, but when he did, he went off. One time, when I was 6, I accidentally dropped a plate of food in front of the TV. That made him mad, and he began to whip me with his belt buckle. He was hitting me and hitting me and my mom yelled, "Stop! That's it! That's it!" But he kept on until he felt like stopping. He whipped me like I was a man.

I never forgot that. I still resent him for that whipping because I didn't deserve a beating for dropping a plate of food. He went overboard with me because, deep down, he's scared to lose control. He's often said that he wants to make sure that no one can take advantage of him again.

When my father goes off, I feel like every word I hear from his mouth is a dagger going into me.

He grew up on the streets, where a lot of people got over on him. I think that's why he's scared to let his guard down now.

I grew up feeling scared in my house. I didn't feel like I could say or do anything that my father didn't approve of. If I was writing in the same room where he was watching TV, he'd tell me, "Look at this" or "Look at that." I couldn't do my own thing in peace.

I hated when he was home because the smallest things could set him off. Once, we were watching basketball on TV and he complimented one of the player's shots. I disagreed because I thought the player could've done it differently. He barked back, "When you get the experience I have, then say something." I let it go, but sometimes I argued back. But it was his house, and I wasn't an adult.

One day, my mom couldn't take his abuse anymore. When I was 12, she ran away with me to Jersey City to be near her relatives in our own apartment.

I was so happy being away from him. I felt like chains had fallen off me. I could kick back and do simple things like write wherever I wanted to write and speak freely. Before, I couldn't say things that were "wrong" without having my head cut off by my pops.

But he soon started calling my mom because he wanted to get back with her. After a few weeks, she told me that she wanted to give it another try. I said that I didn't want us to go back because I felt free. But my mother persisted. She said she would go on her own terms and make sure that he wouldn't hit her anymore. So, after a few months, we moved back in with my father. And he stopped hitting her.

But even though my father was wrong for hitting my mom in the first place, he blames her for walking out. He says that she embarrassed him to his family by leaving him and he's angry with her. And as far as I know, he's never asked forgiveness for what he did to her.

As I became a teenager, things didn't improve with me and my dad. He had tantrums often, and continued to carry a lot of hostility. Everything was aggressive about him, even the way he brushed his teeth.

I've had to deal with his foul mouth and nasty temper when I've dared to disagree with him. One time when we were walking down the street, when I was 17, he told me how I better not think I could kick his butt just because I'm getting older and stronger.

I was like, "How you gonna talk like that? That isn't gonna

happen."

And he said, "Yeah, I'm just letting you know 'cause a lot of guys now don't respect their elders, and when they get older and get power they think they can put something over on them."

I was so mad. It seemed like he was taking his insecurities out on me. I threw my can of soda into the trash in anger. He said, "You better watch yourself!" And I yelled back, "I just threw it! That's all!"

"Don't go there with me," he said. "I swear to God I will put your head right through that plate glass window. You don't know me, motherf-cker, you don't know me! I swear I'll f-cking fling your ass through the window and go home and take out your moms and disappear." People were glancing at us. I didn't say anything, but I was hurt and offended. On the train ride home, I cried.

My pops just stood off to the side. I think he pretended that he didn't notice. I never forgot that threat. And I've never forgiven him for saying it. When my father goes off, I feel like every word I hear from his mouth is a dagger going into me. I feel hotter and hotter, like a volcano about to explode. My chest expands, and I get full of emotions waiting to burst out. So I channel it into something positive. I go into my room and write what I'm feeling. I refuse to let his anger and fear infect me.

He's insecure. He needs to feel in control. He needs help. But how do you tell that to a person like him?

My father just doesn't seem to get it. His actions and threats are a result of his issues that he needs to work on. He's insecure. He needs to feel in control. He needs help. But how do you tell that to a person like him? He's never asked for forgiveness for the things he's done. To me, that shows that he doesn't see his mistakes, so he won't change.

One time, I tried talking to him after an argument. I told him that I felt like he was attacking me and not listening to me when he said some of the things he said. He was like, "Why are you threatened by me? I say a lot of things, but they're just empty threats. When someone gets angry, they start saying crazy things," adding that he loves me and my mom. But my father's aggressive actions and words still bother me because he shouldn't verbally abuse me, especially if he loves me.

I t's hard to feel like he even supports me. My mom was jumping for joy when I started writing for Youth Communication, but he said and did nothing.

My father has occasionally shown his approval of things I've done, like when I make a touchdown, or when I managed to get to safety when a gun was pulled on me in junior high. But then he'll forget about these things when he has a point to make. After I turned 18, he said, "You better stop hanging on your mother's skirt and start to fend for yourself."

I think to myself, "How could he say that when I've proven I can handle myself even without my mom?" It's like he's scared and wants to hold everyone in a lower position than himself just so he can feel powerful.

But despite living with my overbearing pops, I've developed a will of my own. I think it's because my mother gave me support and allowed me to feel free and think for myself. And despite his bullying, my father has told me one thing that I live by. He has a motto: "If 50 people believe in one thing and you believe in another with all your heart, then stick to your guns."

He told me to do what I think is right, like stay away from drugs and stay true to what I believe in and not to be intimidated. I grew up believing in these things, which is how I gathered the courage to stand up to him.

The last time my father tried to bully me, I let him know that I wasn't going to take it. I was 18, and my father, my older brother Felix, and I were watching basketball. He wanted to show my brother a move, so he told me to get up and demonstrate.

I said I was tired and didn't want to, and he insisted. I knew that my not doing as he said was asking for something to happen, but I didn't care. He said he was sick of me. "I'm gonna lift you from that chair," he shouted. I yelled back at him. Then, he got up and started choking me.

And I jumped up and at him. I was mad. I felt possessed! Felix grabbed me and held me back. My father looked almost shocked. My brother told me to go into my room. What I wanted to tell my father was that I am not mom and I won't take his abuse. But my brother closed the door to my room and told me to cool off.

My father was so mad. I could hear him saying how I ain't gonna disrespect him like that, that he'll beat the sh-t out of me. He was yelling at mom, asking how she let me get like this. Eventually, we both cooled off before things got more out of hand. After that day, my pops has chilled with his threats. He hasn't gone off on me since then, 'cause he knows I'll stick up for myself. Nor does he attempt to touch me. I'm not scared of him anymore.

When I get a sense that my dad's gonna come into my room or try to talk to me, I just leave.

Because we live in the same house, though, I still have to deal with his efforts to control me. I try to minimize the amount of time I interact with my father when I'm at home by keeping my room door closed, only coming out for food and water. But sometimes he just storms in, usually finding something to move around. He tells me the frame on my picture is not the right way, or to turn off my radio.

After my experiences with my dad, when I get a sense that he's gonna come into my room or try to talk to me, I just leave. I don't want to get into confrontations. I prefer to just walk away.

I plan on moving as soon as I get a job. I want to get a small apartment, even if it's a room, where I know I won't be bothered by him. I want to disconnect myself from him.

I also want to leave because of my mom. I think I'm the glue that keeps them together in some ways. My mom wants to be in the Dominican Republic with her own mother, but she also thinks of me and my interests. So maybe if I'm on my own, she'll feel free to leave too.

I'm tired of my pops. I'm not gonna act like I respect him, and be scared of him like he wants me to be. To live in my household is to know the daily pressure of his constant loudness and aggressiveness and in-your-faceness.

It's not worth talking to him any more. I've had my say. I'm done.

The writer was 20 when he wrote this story.

Karolina Zaniesienko

Long-Distance Dad

By Dahyana Orozco

When I was little, my mother used to tell me, "You smile just like your father." People who knew him would see me and say, "Your eyes are just like your father's. You look so alike." It made me happy when they said that. Even though I didn't remember much what my father looked like or acted like, I felt like I could look in the mirror and see some of him reflected in me. But ever since my mom and I moved to the United States to join my father when I was 12, I see mostly our differences.

My father left Colombia to come to the U.S. when I was 5. Soon my memories of him faded, so I only knew him from what people told me, the letters he wrote me, and our phone conversations.

When we talked on the phone, on weekends and sometimes during the week, I'd run out of things to tell him. We'd talk about school and he'd ask me what I wanted for Christmas or for my birthday. Somehow it sounded like we were forced to talk to each other—I didn't know what to say and he'd stay quiet, too.

Still, I just thought it was hard to connect over the phone and that we'd be close once we were back together. Every time I had a nightmare, I wished he were there with me. Sometimes I felt angry that he wasn't. My mother tried to be both mom and dad, but I wanted him to protect me, give me advice, even scream at me when I needed it.

My mother used to tell me how good-looking my father was, and how romantic and sweet he had been. She told me about their first date and first kiss, and I imagined him like a prince. I thought that when we finally lived together, he would hold me and lift me up like my friends' fathers used to do to them.

So I was excited when my mother, my sister Lina, and I moved to the U.S. to live with my father when I was 12. My biggest dream was to be with my father and be together as a family.

But moving also meant leaving my friends and home behind, and when I arrived in the U.S. that first night, I was feeling so down and lonely. My father, cousins, aunts, and uncles had all gathered to welcome me, but they didn't feel like family. They felt like strangers—even my father.

When he saw me, he looked surprised. He hugged me for a few seconds and then said, "You don't look like the little girl I left seven years ago in Colombia." I just smiled without knowing what to do. I felt confused because I didn't know if he was proud or disappointed.

The next day, I felt totally lost. I missed my friends, my house, even the annoying sounds of the cars that used to wake me up in the morning back in Pereira, Colombia. Suddenly the excitement that I had been feeling about coming here became frustration and disappointment.

It soon seemed like my father was frustrated and disappointed too. He seemed bothered by our presence. When I helped my mother clean and organize things before he came back from work, he'd say to me, "Why can't you leave everything as it is? Now I won't know where anything is." It made me feel like an intruder.

He used to yell at my mother, "You don't know how to cook!" or "You put too much salt in it." Then he would eat it all. That made me so mad. I wanted to tell him how ungrateful he was, but I didn't want to make things worse. He wasn't acting like the sweet man my mother had told me about.

I wasn't surprised that when I got to high school and started dating, my father had a fit.

He and my mother fought every day, and that upset me. I thought, "How can my mother stand my dad for so long? Why doesn't she divorce him?" I felt like I shouldn't have thought about my father that way, but I could see that my mother suffered, even though she said she was OK.

He and I had many fights too, mostly about my social life and boyfriends. Even though I missed my old friends in Colombia, I made many new ones here. But my father didn't seem to like my friends, not even the girls. He especially hated it when guys called me. Sometimes he'd sit right beside me to listen to my conversation. I'd tell my friends that I'd call them later when he wasn't home.

I wasn't surprised that when I got to high school and started dating, my father had a fit. When my mom told him about it, he got mad at me and said, "Who do you think you are? You are too young to date. Are you going to fall so easily for a guy's lines?"

I thought he sounded absurd; he was talking to me as if he had never dated or liked someone before. It was hard to understand his concern when all I felt was his anger and distrust.

My mother, though, was supportive, and she gave me advice. I talked about my father with her, and she asked me to understand him. She said she knew what I was going through and that it was a difficult period for all of us because we were getting to know each other.

Afterward, I tried talking with my father. After lots of talks and promises that I was not going to do anything I wasn't ready to do, like having sex, he finally understood that dating is normal.

Still, my father says I dress too sexy because I wear tight jeans and skirts, and he doesn't like that I listen to Eminem. He also doesn't get it that a lot of the guys I talk to are just my friends.

I lost my fantasy father, and it's frustrating to have to deal with the real one.

I feel like it's too late for him to act like the bossy parent. I know it's not his fault he wasn't around to tell me what to do when I was younger. He was working here to support our family. But I resent that my father feels he can tell me how to act.

I think everything would have been easier if we hadn't spent so much time apart. If I'd grown up with him, maybe he'd understand me better and I wouldn't feel so angry at him.

It hurt me most that he seemed to be trying to push everybody away and pretend he didn't need us. Usually I acted like I wasn't bothered by it, but I once showed him how I felt.

"You're an ungrateful person," I told him angrily. "You should appreciate your family because you don't know what you've got until you lose it." He looked mad when I said that, but stayed quiet.

After that, whenever he started to get mad about something, I pretended that he was right. I was so tired of always fighting that I decided to give up. I just wanted to live in peace.

I still feel like there is a wall between us, but now that I've been here for almost six years, my relationship with my father has slowly improved. He's not as grouchy, and we don't argue as much.

Sometimes I still feel disappointed that my father is not how I'd imagined him when I was little, but I'm trying to accept him as he is. Maybe he's been going through the same thing. After all, I'm not the little girl he had in his mind. Maybe he's trying to accept me as I am, too.

I hope we can make up for the time we weren't together. I'd like to grow up with him in my life. I want my father to be there for my college graduation, my wedding, my first child.

Even though he makes me angry and frustrated sometimes, I love my father. He is a very responsible and courageous person. He never stopped sending my family money while we were in Colombia. He worked long hours while he lived here all alone, leaving at 6 in the morning and coming back at 6 in the evening. I am grateful for all the sacrifices he has made for me.

Sometimes I'd like to hug him and tell him how much he means to me, but I'm afraid to do it. I don't think he'd ignore me or push me away, but it would be awkward. I'm worried that he doesn't love me back in the same way, and even if he does, he probably won't show it.

I feel sad knowing that I lost my fantasy father. It's frustrating to have no choice but to deal with the real one, especially when the real one is not what I expected. I'm resigned to it, but I haven't given up hope that we can have a better relationship.

Dahyana was 18 when she wrote this story.

Sara Goldys

Dealing With An Absent Dad

Dr. Neil Altman is a therapist and author of the book The Analyst in the Inner City: Race, Class, and Culture Through a Psychoanalytic Lens. *Here, he talks about what good fathers give and how fatherless teenagers can get those things from other people.*

Q: What does a good father give boys, and can other people provide it?

A: If you're a boy, then a father has a special role in shaping your sense of what it means to be a man. Ideas of manhood are changing, but there are still expectations that boys and men will be less emotional and more tough.

Having an older man you respect in your life, even if he's not your dad, is important because he brings those expectations of manhood down to human size. This real man shows you that nobody can be perfectly tough or unemotional. You learn from the cracks in his façade. Seeing a father or mentor react to an emotional challenge in a good way just one time can teach a kid something.

Q: What about girls?

A: For girls, fathers are particularly important in adolescence. Sometimes a father and daughter who've been close when she was younger will retreat from each other when she hits puberty. Girls often feel awkward around all older men as their bodies change.

The culture is so focused on young females as sex objects that it's just as important for the girl as for the boy to get a positive male role model at that point—one who sees women as people. A girl needs to have a model of males in her life who are interested in her as a thinking and feeling person.

Q: Where can a fatherless kid find role models?

A: Seek out environments that help you develop yourself, and you'll find people who can show you the things you need. A church, for example, is both a community center and a bunch of caring people. Go where you can use any special talent you have, like making art or doing sports. Sports can help you grow because you have to cope

Seek out environments that help you develop yourself, and you'll find people who can show you the things you need.

with losing, which makes it an emotional outlet. Music is another great way of connecting to feelings.

You'll find mentors and role models in environments where you can express emotion. And an adult you talk to but don't live with can provide you with a calmer place, a different point of view, someone to talk to who won't throw what you told them back in your face 24/7. These are some of the same things a father provides in a traditional household where the mother is with the children a lot more.

Q: How can you prepare for meeting a father who's been gone a long time?

A: Read *Dreams From My Father* by Barack Obama! Notice how Obama pays attention to the conflicting things he feels when he meets his father for the first time, and how he sorts all that out (see pp. 63-70 in the paperback). Understand that your father feels guilty and that you're going to feel angry and hopeful. There's going to be love or potential love on both sides. You can't make the guilt and anger go away.

Your father may want you to understand why he wasn't there for you. You won't feel understanding at first—that will have to evolve over time. But don't tell him everything you need at that first meeting. I think it's best at an initial meeting to be low-key and just find out how each person is feeling.

Talk to someone else about your feelings at first. Process that first meeting with that trusted person. Your father feels vulnerable and guilty and ashamed and worries he'll be misunderstood; he's probably not ready to hear your feelings. (It's OK if your feelings do slip out, though.) After two or three meetings, you could maybe bring up some of your own feelings.

But first, you, the son or daughter, have to admit to yourself what you need from him. You're probably thinking, "I don't need him," because that's how you've coped with his absence.

Q: How do you know what you need from him if you've never had it?

A: There are clues to what you need in what you've been trying to get. As a boy, have you been drawn to gangs? To older guys who seem confident and tough? As a girl, have you been attracted to older guys of a particular type, maybe who have money? If you've been looking for it in positive places—meaning people who care about you and are reliable—that's great, that means you're more comfortable with needing it.

If you don't believe you can ever get that kind of positive

attention, then your longing for it gets a little twisted. You could end up denying you need anything while seeking it out at the same time.

Q: What do you need to watch out for if you're reuniting with your dad after he's been out of your life?

A: You need to find out something about your father, and the older you are, the easier this gets. What's his life like? Why does he want to see you now? Can you figure that out when you talk to him? Does he seem more mature now than he did when you were little? Is he feeling so guilty and defensive that he won't be able to handle it when you start to tell him you've been hurt and angry?

People develop fantasies of absent parents. You may be expecting somebody wonderful, but what you'll get is a complicated human.

Meanwhile the people who have taken care of you—foster parents, a mother or other relative—have let you down in small ways, restricted your movements, and made you angry. You may be tempted to defy whoever's been taking care of you and think, "My father's going to swoop down and take me to a better life."

People develop fantasies of absent parents. You may be expecting somebody wonderful, but what you'll get is a complicated human with lots of problems as well as some good qualities.

Q: Is there anything else you'd say to people who grew up without fathers?

A: I think kids who are without their biological parents—both mothers and fathers—are prone to thinking that if only they had them they would be OK. And that's not true. Biological parents come with all kinds of problems, and yes, they help, but it's not a dealbreaker for your life if you don't have them.

Bryan Lindsay

Invisible Man

By Onician Wood

My father left before I was born, leaving my mother to be a single parent, and me to be plagued by a feeling of abandonment. I felt short-changed. I hated that he wasn't there to pick me up when I fell down or to congratulate me at my graduations.

As a teenager, I had bitter moments where curses echoed in my mind whenever I thought about him. I flat-out hated the man. Sometimes I blamed him for the difficult times I went through.

According to my Aunt Renee, my mother and father, who were never married, broke up because my mother discovered he was cheating. After their separation, my mother learned that she was pregnant with me. My father found out that she was expecting, but didn't take responsibility for his actions.

My mother was petrified of telling her parents because my grandfather was a minister and, according to the Bible, having a child out of wedlock is a sin. My mother revealed her secret to Aunt Renee, and Renee soon announced to my grandparents that my mother was pregnant. But despite my mother's fears, my grandparents gave me their unconditional love after I was born, even though I was an illegitimate child.

But hard times were coming. A year after my birth, my mother was diagnosed with lupus. Lupus is a disease where the immune system attacks the body tissue for unknown reasons. The disease took a toll on my mother. She was in and out of the hospital and constantly going to the doctor.

I felt so lonely. I threw the football as high as I could and then sprinted across the yard to catch it.

My mother was an art professor at a university and worked long hours doing lectures and lesson plans. Due to my mother's job and endless doctor appointments, my grandparents babysat me a lot. So did my uncle, who lived with my mother, grandparents, and me.

My uncle didn't get along with my mother. They argued frequently, bickering over petty things. Sometimes I saw my uncle push her. But when she needed him to look after me, he came through.

My uncle was the closest person I ever had to a father. He treated me like I was his own child, which eased my feelings of abandonment. My uncle taught me many things about being a man, instilling in me many of the ethics I have today. He told me to never call women names and to never hit them.

But my uncle had ways that stopped me from idolizing him. In addition to shoving my mother and their constant verbal jousts, he was an alcoholic. His drinking scared me because most of the fights he had with my mother were when he was intoxicated. And sometimes he drank while driving.

My uncle had already been in a minor car accident, and I often worried that he would get in another one because of his drinking and driving. I learned from his mistakes, which is why

I don't drink, do drugs, or push or hit women.

Though my uncle spent countless hours with me, he also had a child of his own, a marriage, and a job to tend to and couldn't be there for me all the time. And though my grandparents were home most of the time to watch me, they were too old to play with me in the front yard.

So I ended up playing football by myself. I felt so lonely. I threw the football as high as I could into the air and then sprinted across the yard to catch it, but I never made it there in time. I taught myself everything I know about sports by reading books or by observing the pros play. I even taught myself how to ride a bike, while constantly falling off of it and crashing into mailboxes, fences, and parked cars.

It was not only painful physically, but emotionally as well, because sports and learning how to ride a bike are things I felt a father should teach his child.

When I was 4 or 5, my mother took me to the park on weekends and I saw kids playing with their fathers. I played by myself because my mother was exhausted from her illness. That's when the feeling of abandonment hit me. There I was, throwing a football to myself while another kid was tossing the pigskin around with his pops. My resentment towards my father flared.

When I was 8, my mother's illness took a turn for the worse. We were walking back to the car after a lecture we attended and she had a seizure. The ambulance rushed her to the emergency room. She was put in intensive care. Eight months after she had the seizure, she died. I felt like part of me died with her. She had awarded guardianship of me to Aunt Renee, who lived in another city.

When my aunt was putting me in the car to drive to the airport, I kicked and screamed because I didn't want to leave my family and friends. After I got to my aunt's house, she enrolled me in a Quaker private school.

I had the new kid blues. I was shy and felt like a social outcast despite the warm welcome my class gave me. I had a southern accent and some of the kids treated me differently because they saw me as "country."

But when people discovered that I was good in sports, everybody wanted me on their team. If not for that, I probably never would've fit in. When my classmates asked me about my parents, I told them, "My mother died from lupus when I was 8, and my father…he…he left before I was born." I felt like I was the special kid. After they found out, they said things like, "I don't know what I'd do without my mother," or asked me questions about how I got by without my father.

I saw myself as a normal kid, but some people treated me like I was disadvantaged because I didn't have a father and had lost my mother. They let me go ahead of them in line to get a snack or shoot first when we played basketball, saying, "Oh, let Onician go first. He doesn't have a father."

I saw myself as a normal kid, but some people treated me like I was disadvantaged because I didn't have a father.

And when people mentioned parents or fathers, they became cautious around me. Some kids said, "Oh, I'm sorry, I forgot you don't have a father." When people kept asking me about my father or apologizing, it really got to me. Most of the kids in the school knew their fathers, which made me feel like an outcast.

I felt like I was the only one in the world who didn't have his father in his life. But I tucked that feeling deep inside myself, never talking about it. I didn't feel as bad when they asked about my mother because I had memories of her. But my father was like French—foreign to me. I didn't know anything about him.

I didn't know where his side of the family was from or if he had other kids. Questions ranging from "What does he look like?" to "What is he like?" sailed through my mind, leaving me shipwrecked in uncertainty about not only who he was, but who I was.

I left the Quaker school after 6th grade and entered a Catholic school. The feeling of being the only child without a father didn't leave me. But it did simmer down because people at my new school didn't make a big deal out of me not having a father and didn't ask about it so much.

The feeling finally faded when I started high school. I met kids who didn't know their fathers or who were abandoned by them. This comforted me a little. But after I saw how many people were without fathers, I was disturbed. I realized that absent fathers in the black community is a major problem. It's right up there with AIDS, poverty, and violence. But I didn't talk to any of my peers about it because I was shy.

I set standards for myself by rebelling against what my father represents to me, which is a deadbeat, a coward, and a cheater.

Then, when I was 15, I read a book given to me by my best friend's mother about young men growing up without fathers. It had short passages of fatherly advice. After finishing the book, I felt like I'd received some life guidance. I also decided to do a book report on it for class.

My best friend's mother knew the author of the book. So I called the author to ask if he could come to my English class for my project, and he agreed. After he spoke, people in class started to talk about not having their fathers and how it affected them. I found out that others felt like I did. I felt enlightened.

After class, the author and I had a long conversation about how we grew up without our fathers and what that meant for us. I felt relieved to finally speak to someone about this problem. I started analyzing my feelings toward the man I referred to as "a figment of a father." I knew there was a lot of anger inside me, but I hadn't addressed it.

Anger and hate are like termites. They start eating away at you, destroying your happiness and causing you to become cold.

Sometimes when I looked in the mirror, I could see this heartless person start to emerge. I realized the animosity I felt toward him only harmed me. He wasn't feeling a drop of the pain I had inside. There was no use in hating him because he's my father. And in a backwards way, he's had the biggest impact on my view of life.

I set standards for myself by rebelling against what he represents to me, which is a deadbeat, a coward, a cheater, and other words I won't use in this story.

One of the biggest rules I've laid down for myself is that I won't have sex with a woman I don't love or whom I wouldn't considering marrying. If anything happens and the girl gets pregnant, I want to be able to say that she's someone who I want to raise my child with.

Another rule is that I'll always be faithful to the woman I'm with because I never want to put another woman through the same thing my mother went through, no matter how attractive the other person is. It's more than a matter of being true to the woman—it's also being respectful to her, which is part of what my uncle taught me.

Now when I reflect back on my childhood and adolescence without my father, I realize that maybe it's for the best that he wasn't there. I don't believe he would've filled the shoes of what a father should be, based on how he handled my mother's pregnancy. By not having him in my life, I became a stronger person, adopting a perspective that makes me strive to be someone who's thoughtful and caring.

Onician was 17 when he wrote this story.
After high school, he went to Bard College.

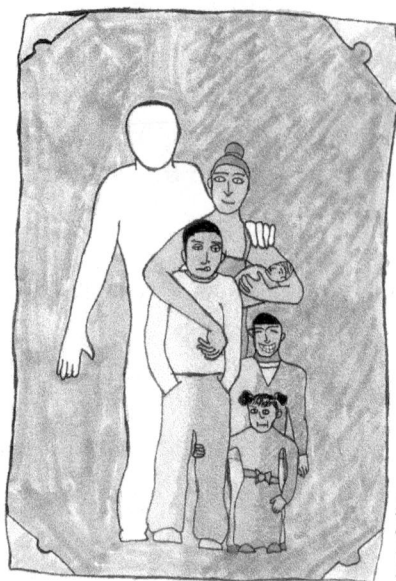

Amir Solimon

Some POPS Are Hanging In

By Antwaun Garcia

One day when I was about 8 or 9, my dad and I were walking down West 125th Street in Harlem, in New York City. A girl walked past and he bet me $5 he could get her phone number. He talked to her and came back with a lipstick kiss on his cheek and a paper with her name and number on it.

"Where's my money?" he asked me.

My father was living with my mother, sister, two brothers and me then, but I knew he wasn't much of a family man. He was always in and out of prison. He would show up and then disappear for two or three years—the same routine over and over. I missed having a dad to help me learn how to read and write, to play sports with and talk to. I wanted him to help me answer questions such as, "Can I make it in life?" and, "What is my purpose?" I've constantly thought to myself, "Why didn't he want any part of me?"

I'm not alone in missing a dad. More than half of all black children don't live with their fathers, according to the U.S. Census Bureau. And at least one in four Hispanic kids and one in five white kids live without their dads. I thought the numbers would be even worse. So many people I know don't have a father.

To better understand why so many men are not taking care of their kids, I went to a program called POPS (Providing Opportunity for Parental Success) in Harlem. POPS works mostly with black and Latino fathers who are 18 to 35 years old. The eight-week workshop helps fathers reunite and connect with their children, and POPS also offers counseling, mediation with family members, and legal help.

POPS doesn't give up on guys and tells them not to give up on having a good relationship with their kids, even if a dad is told he can't see his kids or feels the kid doesn't appreciate him, said Robert Sanchez, the program manager. Once a man participates in POPs, he can come back for help throughout his entire life. "We're like a leech. We latch on and don't let go," Sanchez said.

The program tells fathers not to give up on having a good relationship with their kids.

Sanchez struck me as cool and relaxed, but I found he could relate in a personal way to breaking the cycle of fatherlessness. He caught me off guard because he was dressed in a suit, but actually, he had a little bit of the hood in him. Sanchez didn't get to know his own father, "a dope fiend and alcoholic," until he was 15 years old. And he struggled to stay connected to his own daughter during the 15 years when he was in prison.

Research shows that kids who don't have dads are much more likely to be poor, be depressed, fail school, commit crimes, have sex early on, and (for girls) get pregnant. Why would a man put his kids at such risk? The main reason, Sanchez said, is fear. Having a child is scary! A lot of guys worry that they don't know how to care for a child and don't want to look stupid.

Some men don't stay because of baby mama drama. "Fifty percent of our fathers have a volatile relationship with their child's mother," and almost none are married to them, he noted. Frustrated with their child's mother, men may stop seeing their kids to avoid fights and conflict. Or, the mothers may not let them visit.

Other dads disappear because they get caught up in the streets or prison. And lots of fathers have no idea how to be a good parent because they never had one themselves. At least 15% of the men who participate in POPS were in foster care when they were boys, Sanchez said.

Many men believe a father's only role is to provide for their children. Men with jobs are more likely to be present in their children's lives. Those without money often don't stick around because they "associate fatherhood as an extension of their pocket, and think 'I'll stay out of the child's life until I have money,'" Sanchez explained.

But even the poorest fathers can support their children in important ways, Sanchez said. A father is not just a roll of bills, but "a guiding light, a teacher, a friend, a protector, an enlightener. A father is a supporter, someone you can go to for understanding and love.

"One question I ask fathers is, 'What is one great thing you remember about your dad?" Their answers, Sanchez said, never have to do with how much money their fathers spent on them. "That child is not going to remember the sneakers, but he does remember the time you took him to the park, or to a baseball game, or made him feel good about himself."

Real fatherhood, said Sanchez, is "if you gave them a hug every day," spent time with them, and showed you really cared about their feelings. In POPS, dads learn how to hold a newborn and how a baby communicates his needs by crying. POPS shows men how easy it is to play with their children, help them with homework, ask about their interests, or discover something new by taking them on outings. Dads learn child development, how to be patient, and how to solve a child's problems without criticizing a child or making her feel bad.

More than half of all black children don't live with their fathers.

If the mother won't let a dad see his kids, POPS workers take the dad to family court and show him how to establish paternity, get a visitation order, and enforce his legal rights to see his children.

Sanchez's own history explains why he is so passionate about fatherhood. At 18, Sanchez fathered a daughter. He was also arrested in an apartment where drugs were found and sent to prison for 15 years. While incarcerated, he wrote to his daughter, saw her on visits, and kept communication open with his daughter's mother.

When he came out of prison, his feelings were hurt because he bought his daughter a cellphone to stay in touch with him but she didn't call him much. Then one day he watched a Spanish flick, "Mi Familia," that showed a character returning from prison and trying to force his child into a relationship. The child rejects him. An older, wiser relative tells the man, "You can't come home and demand a relationship."

"That, to me, was a lesson," said Sanchez.

The movie helped him understand that fathers must be patient and that it takes children a long time to learn to trust someone who left them. His daughter was a little afraid he would make new rules for her and try to control her, Sanchez explained. "Her feelings were legitimate. I had been out of her life for 14 years and had to give her space and room to feel what she was feeling."

Sanchez let his daughter know he would always be there for her, but that she could have some say in how much time they would spend together. Now they see each other about twice a month, when she comes to New York. (She lives in Massachusetts.) "She's in a rebellious stage and a father is the perfect person to be rebellious against," Sanchez explained.

When Sanchez was released from prison, he made friends with people he trusted to help him out when he felt stuck or confused. "I made it my business to know what a father was, with positive fathers and role models around me."

He encourages dads at POPS to search for mentors to help them. A good role model is someone who is accountable (shows up when he says he will and keeps his promises), takes responsibility when he makes mistakes (admits he's wrong, apologizes, and makes amends), and knows how to listen without criticizing. Once you find one, "tell him that you admire him and ask if he can give you guidance," Sanchez advised.

In order to be a good father, you need to understand your own anger, your past, and your parents.

In order to be a good father, you need to understand your own anger, your past, and your parents, Sanchez explained. Sanchez wanted to break his own family's cycle of father absence so badly he was willing to do things that were new and uncomfortable for him, like not using drugs or alcohol, forgiving people who wronged him, going back to school (he earned a master's degree in urban theology), and traveling all over the world.

I always believed that it was easy for some fathers to give up on raising their children. Now I know that there are fathers, like Sanchez and those in POPS and other fatherhood programs, who are out there trying to stay in the lives of their children. They want to break the cycle. When it's my turn I'm going to try to break mine as well.

Antwaun was 20 when he wrote this story.

Martell Brown

Saying Goodbye
to My Superman

By Griffin Kinard

My father died of AIDS when I was 9. Man, I remember the first day I saw him in the hospital. My brothers and I walked through the doors of my father's resting place. We waited to see him. Some people came down the hall with a man in a wheelchair. They pushed this man into the room I was in. He was looking all out of shape, real skinny, as if the hospital was not feeding him.

My father is in shape, very big and muscular. As a child, I feared him. So I thought, "This is a mix-up. This man is not my father." But he was.

My father was in a wheelchair. He was so weak he could not beat me anymore. I was very confused. I would never in a million years have thought that my father could be defenseless.

For 20 minutes I was stuck on stupid. I was mesmerized and

a little stunned. Seeing my father all discombobulated like that, no lie, revenge was on my mind. I did not know whether to hit my father or hug him. But despite all the things my father did to me I could never raise my hand up at my old man.

So I hugged him, and my father, my brothers, and I had a nice little conversation. I don't remember now what we were talking about. It was just random things off the tops of our heads, but it made me feel good.

I lived with both of my parents until I was 3 or 4. My father was the man of the house and he made his presence known. My mother was doing a lot of running because of my father's abusive ways.

I do not know where my father's violent behavior came from, but I think he was abused as a youth himself. Because I was so young, I've never been able to figure him out.

All I remember about my dad was that he was pure chaos. Sometimes everything you did was wrong. If you were up after my dad came home you got beat. If you did not finish your food you got beat. Nothing but pain, inexcusable pain. It was like a war zone in my house. There was nothing but tension. Beat-downs were everywhere. Nobody was spared.

Eventually, my mother left and my siblings and I came into care when the system got sick of my dad abusing us. When I got into care, my family and I were all separated. I was sent to three foster homes, then to the New York Foundling Hospital, then to Children's Village, a residential treatment center where I lived for most of my childhood.

I thought, "This is a mix-up. This man is not my father." But he was.

For some odd reason, I never hated my dad. I saw my dad as my Superman and my Lex Luthor; he was everything I loved and feared.

When I was taken from home my father was the only one I really wanted to see. He came to visit me at Children's Village on the regular. We had fun. He brought me candy and books, and I was always surprised to see him. I wanted to go back home, but I didn't realize at that time that that was a far-fetched dream.

When my dad got sick, it felt like my Superman was leaving me. I visited my father every day in the hospital, knowing that one day I would not see him again. The man that caused all this pain to my family and me was leaving for good. I shed tears.

Counting down to my father's death was the most horrible feeling in the world, but as the days and months went on, I still visited my father at his pit stop to the heavens.

The hospital people were very good to my father, and that was weird to me, but what really caught my attention was how nice my father was. It was like the monster inside my father was dying quicker than he was.

My father became more of a listener and storyteller. We laughed, played, and took pictures. That time with my father was really something to remember. My father was showing his emotions, and that was something that he did not do. I knew that in some spiritual kind of way my father was a new man.

The same man who used to abuse me showed me that it is never too late to change.

I would have never guessed it, but the same man who used to abuse me showed me that it is never too late to change.

Toward the end of my father's life, he became determined to let his kids know how he truly felt about us. I did not think he could do it, but he did. He told us that he loved us, and that we needed to stay together, and to always remember that there is a place after here—where you go, that's up to you.

Those were the last words that my father ever said to me, and man, I'll never forget them.

On December 4, I was getting ready to take a shower when I decided to make a phone call to my grandmother. The minute I got on the phone with her she told me that my father had passed. I knew this day would come. I knew it was only a matter of time, but I still wasn't ready.

I did not go to my father's funeral. Saying goodbye is very hard for me.

Even though my father has passed, he will always be with me. I am beginning to understand that my father's spirit lives within me and he is guiding me to the promised land. I cannot wait to see what it looks like.

Griffin was 20 when he wrote this story.

Martha Riley Willis

My Father, My Friend

By Macario DeLaCruz

It's said that everybody has a double in the world who they'll probably never meet. Well, I've met mine. I've known him all my life. No, he's not my twin, but he is my reflection.

Or maybe I'm his. I'm speaking about my father—the lighter, older, and shorter version of me. Or am I the darker, younger, and taller version of him? When I let my hair grow, even though it's curlier than his, I look just like he did at my age. Our temperaments and personalities are similar, too. We're both laid-back, realistic, and good-natured guys. We don't get angry much, though we do get annoyed quickly.

When we're thinking deeply we both rub our thumb and pointer finger across our bottom lip and fold our hands in front of our face the same way. And we can both wiggle our ears. He's just like me—really. It's weird, yet cool—I think.

I don't live with my dad. My parents separated when I was 6 or 7. I live with my mother and brother in Brooklyn, New York. But I see my dad, who lives by himself in Manhattan, often. My parents generally get along fine. They just can't live each other. My dad visits us in Brooklyn whether my mom is home or not.

But most of the time I see him when I go to Manhattan and hook up with him there. Usually it's just to get a bite to eat, but sometimes we'll go to the movies or shopping for games, books, CDs, DVDs, or clothes. And I can call him any time.

Even though we don't live together (or maybe because we don't), we're very close. I can talk to him about everything— sports, video games, politics, music, life, rain, computers (even though he doesn't know much about them), writing, yoga, fish, or anything. No topic is taboo.

I admire my dad a lot as well. If I had to describe him with one word, it would be "sage." He's highly intelligent and wise. He tells you what you need to hear. The general theme of his advice is: "Put the work in if you want to get anything out of it and accomplish things in life."

People who see us together often think we're friends and not father and son. The other day, my dad and I stopped in a shoe store, and he bought some shoes.

As the cashier rung up the shoes, she and my dad asked each other about their ethnic backgrounds. He told her he was black and Filipino. She said she was American, because she was born here, but she's Chinese because her parents were born there.

Then she asked, "What about your friend?" referring to me. He said laughingly, "That's my son."

She replied, "Yeah, OK," like she didn't believe him. After my dad showed her our IDs (and our same names, Macario DeLaCruz), she remarked that she was astonished by how young my dad looked, and how we looked like friends, or maybe brothers, but not father and son.

When we left the store I jokingly told him, as I often do, "If it wasn't for me, you wouldn't have those good looks, you know." He laughed and smiled, then we grabbed a bite to eat.

I'm not sure why people peg my father and me as friends and not brothers. I think it's probably because even though I think we look alike, I'm much darker than him, my hair isn't like his (mine's curly and long, while his is straight and short), and my frame is bigger than his.

Our relationship is totally different from my friends' relationships with their dads. For one thing, my dad is pretty young. All of my friends' dads are in their 40s, while my dad is 36.

(My mom is young, too. Occasionally, people think we're friends, but 90% of the time they think we're brother and sister.)

I can talk to my dad about everything—sports, video games, politics, music, life, rain, computers, writing, yoga, or fish.

My dad and I also share the same interests, like video games and music. We both like rap, r&b, and hip-hop, and consider Tupac Shakur (2Pac) the greatest rapper of all time. We're also both into Jimi Hendrix.

I know for a fact that my friends' fathers have no interest in listening to rap (and all of its "bad influences") and haven't the remotest interest in playing video games. Their only concern about video games is how much it's going to cost them to buy their kid's next system.

But there are some things about my dad I just don't get. I can't see ever participating in my dad's hideous habit of smoking cigarettes. To give him credit, he's started to cut down, or at least he says he has. And at least he doesn't smell like smoke. I've told him to quit, but I haven't pushed him on it.

It's weird that my dad smokes, which has a terrible effect on the user's lungs, but also does yoga, which helps a person's breathing. As he's always telling me, "Yoga will teach you how to breathe correctly and it will help you focus." I think he's intent on doing yoga to balance out or counteract his smoking habit.

He's tried to get me into yoga, but I'm not very interested. I'll stick to basketball and football and sometimes baseball, but I'll leave yoga for the "old man." It seems more for older people and people who are stressed out, like college students.

As I've gotten older, my dad and I have slowly gotten closer. When we go our separate ways, there's no kiss on the cheek or just a plain ol' "Goodbye," like

When we go our separate ways, there's no kiss on the cheek or plain ol' "Goodbye." Instead, we give each other a pound.

how some of my friends say bye to their fathers. Instead, we give each other a pound. That may seem odd to people who are used to seeing only friends doing that with friends, but to me and my dad, it's second nature. Wouldn't have it any other way.

Macario was 17 when he wrote this story.
He graduated from high school and went to college.

Whitney Harris

Meeting the Invisible Man

By Athena Karoutsos

The last time I saw my father was three years ago, when I was 15. My mom and I had spent the summer in Greece, where he lives. I was about to go back to America and we were sitting in his car, just him and me.

I looked out the window. It was black outside and the dust from the road flew up in the air, making the darkness seem like it was sparkling. I thought of how close my father and I had become that summer. We'd spent almost every day together sitting in cafés drinking European lemonade, going to see other towns, and visiting relatives.

I didn't want to go back to New York and let it be like it had been before. I hadn't seen my father for six years before that summer and this was the first time we'd really spent any time together.

My father could tell I was anxious. "Don't worry. I promise things will change," he said in Greek. "We'll call each other now. If you ever need anything, just tell me and I'll send it to you."

I stayed silent. His words seemed too good to be true. "Why should things change now?" I thought to myself. Still, I wanted to believe him.

As a little kid, I hated Father's Day. When the teacher made us draw cards for our fathers and all the other kids fought over the markers, glitter, and colored paper, I always felt empty inside.

One year when I was about 6, I watched the other kids scribble on the bright paper and felt embarrassed because I had nothing to do. When the teacher asked me why I wasn't joining in, I had to tell her I didn't have a father. She asked me if I knew anyone else who was a father and told me to make a card for them. I made a card for my uncle.

Before that I had never thought of my father. I knew everyone had one but I didn't know exactly what a father was. But now I began to wonder, if everyone else had a father, why didn't I? A few months after the card-making incident, I asked my mom about him.

She told me how she'd gone to visit her family in Greece one summer. When she was on the boat going to the island she's from, Ikaria, she saw my father looking at her. Soon after that they fell in love.

My mom got pregnant with me, and my father told her to live in his apartment while he was away. (He's a first mechanic on boats so he spends half the year at sea.) But my mother didn't want to stay there alone and she needed to come back to America to take care of her mother, who was sick. Besides, she wanted me to be born in New York so I would be a U.S. citizen. So after a few months she went home to New York.

When I was born, my mother called my father and told him I was a girl, but he didn't seem happy. She was so upset that when the hospital staff asked for my father's name for my birth certificate, she left it blank.

He'd never come to see me, but my mom reminded me that I'd met my father once, two years before, when I was 4. She showed me some pictures of us together in his apartment in Athens (the largest city and capital of Greece).

There was one picture of me watching him shave and another of him reading to me while I held a doll. I suddenly remembered how I had left the doll there. I missed the doll and didn't think of anything else. My father seemed like a stranger to me.

Most of the time, I didn't feel anything was missing from my life. My mother gave me whatever I needed and tried her best to give me what I wanted. And I had the rest of my family, too. My aunt and uncle threw me big birthday parties and let me bring my friends to their house in Long Island for the weekend. They bought me toys and gave me ballet lessons. My other uncle took me shopping and even gave me spending money, since my mom often couldn't.

I saw my father again briefly when I was 8 and my mom took me to Greece, but all I remember was pulling my hand away when he tried to hold it and meeting his new wife. After that I didn't see him until we went to Greece again, the summer I turned 15.

By this time I had several friends whose parents weren't together. But their fathers called them and saw them as often as they could, even if they lived in other countries. I never even got one phone call.

For the first time, I wanted to see my father. I wanted to ask him, "Why?" I knew half of myself but I didn't know the other half. I was growing up and I wanted to know myself as a whole. So when my mom told me he was going to be in Ikaria that summer and he wanted to see me, I was glad, though nervous.

B ut once we got to Greece, I felt unsure if I was ready to see him. I was filled with the same uncertainty that I feel when I think about death, that there's no way to know what it's going to be like until it happens.

I watched my father a few times before I met him. The first time, my mom and I were eating on the balcony of a café in Ikaria and my father and his wife passed by down below us. My mom pointed him out to me. Another time I was in a taxi and I passed by him sitting at his sister's restaurant. Each time I couldn't believe it was him. He was so close to me but at the same time so unreachable, like he'd always been.

After a few days, I decided I had to meet him if I was ever going to get any answers. My mother, who wanted me to

He was so close to me but at the same time so unreachable, like he'd always been.

have a relationship with him as much as I did, was relieved. She planned for me to meet him at my aunt's restaurant that night.

Of course he was late. I sat in the restaurant waiting and felt too much all at once—sadness, fear, and hope. When I saw him come in, I felt my heart in my throat. I couldn't move.

He looked nothing like he had in the few photographs I had of him. Age had caught up with him. He'd grown a round belly. His hair was thin and straight, not curly and thick like in the photos. When he smiled, his teeth were yellow and chipped.

He came over to hug me, but I just stood there and wouldn't hug him back. So he shook my hand. My father was shaking and his eyes were wet. I had always thought of him as emotionless. I hadn't thought he might be as nervous about our meeting as I was.

Everyone was staring at us—his wife, my mother, my cousins, my aunt and uncle. He told me to sit down and got me a Sprite. I couldn't speak or drink. I couldn't even feel the cold glass in my hand. Then he asked me to go for a ride in his car so we could be alone to talk.

When we were in the car I wanted to say so many things. He just asked me how I was, how my mom was and how my aunt and uncles were doing. Then I finally burst out, "Why don't you ever call or write to me?"

He sat, thinking. Finally he stuttered, "I tried calling once. Did you change your number? I lost your address."

What shocked me most was how lame his answer was. "Couldn't he at least have had the decency to make up a good excuse?" I thought.

My thoughts raced. "I'm his only child. I don't care if he willingly or unwillingly made me. I am a part of him. How could he abandon a part of him? How could he not even care to know how I was all these years? What if I was suffering? What if I was dead? He wouldn't have known. Did he even care?" I thought. But I said nothing because it was hard enough asking the first question.

We drove back in silence. It hit me that maybe he had no idea how badly he was treating me and if I was ever going to have a relationship with my father I'd have to be the one to do something. Even though I thought he didn't deserve forgiveness, I knew it was the only way for things to change. So inside of me I forgave him.

I ended up having a wonderful summer. I got to spend time with him, which was all that mattered to me. He'd try to buy me things, but I didn't want his money. I just wanted his time. I wanted to know I was worth my father's time.

One day we drove to a town on the other side of the island. We sat down at a restaurant and ordered something to eat. "Do you want some lemonade?" my father struggled to ask in English. His terrible accent was endearing and I laughed. "Why are you laughing? Is it funny how I said that?" he said in Greek, smiling.

"No," I lied, as I tried to control my laughter. Then the food came. We didn't talk, but the silence had become more comfortable.

Though I saw him nearly every day that summer, we never really talked. I learned only a few things about my father, and one was how similar he was to me when it came to expressing emotions out loud. I could tell how my father kept it all inside and I saw regret in his eyes.

But even though there was silence between us, I liked being near my father. It made me feel safe to know that if anything were to happen he was there to protect me, like a father should. I spent every moment I could with him. I even called him "Father," and when I did he would smile. I knew I made my father happy. I felt complete.

I wanted to know I was worth my father's time.

The summer passed by quickly and soon it was time to leave. We sat in his car that one last time and he made his promise—his lie. As soon as I came back to New York I went out in the pouring rain to buy a calling card because I missed my father.

When I called there was that silence between us again. He asked if I was all right and if I needed anything, and then we couldn't think of anything else to say. After that phone call the days went by and he never called. I waited for a letter and it never came.

It's been three years now and I haven't heard from him. Things are just like they were before that visit. Except in a sense it's worse now because I know what I'm missing.

I don't think my father is someone anyone can have any kind of relationship with. He doesn't talk to his own mother and he has gotten divorced from his wife. I think his mind is like a child's and he doesn't know right from wrong. He doesn't realize all the people he's hurting. I feel sorry for him but I'm tired of trying and I don't think I'll try again. It's not worth the pain.

Despite all this, I'm not angry at myself for trusting him. In fact, I still do trust him. There are many ways to trust someone and I trust that though he won't be there for me, he does love me.

Dealing With Dad

I wouldn't take back that summer because it gave me good memories of my father. And even though I don't expect it, I will never stop waiting for him to call.

Athena was 17 when she wrote this story. She graduated from high school and attended the City College of New York.

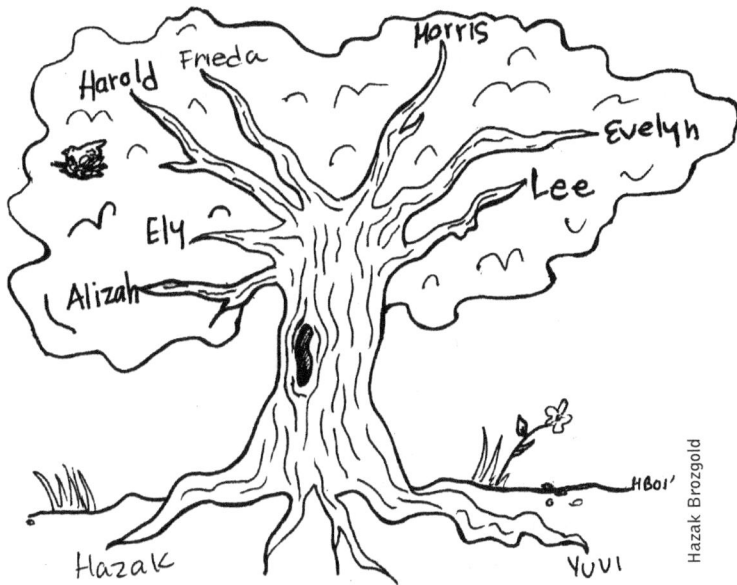

Hazak Brozgold

Tracing My Family Tree

By Hazak Brozgold

"This is a quest," my dad told me, "not only for me, but for you and your brother, for future generations." He wasn't talking about the search for a cure for cancer or AIDS, but about his genealogy research.

Genealogy is the tracing of family history. Lately, my dad's been spending a lot of his spare time trying to fill in the empty spaces on our family tree and re-establishing contacts with relatives we've lost touch with. "Our family origins have always been a great mystery," my father explained, catching my interest.

People are always asking me about my name because it's unusual. When I tell them it's Hebrew, they say, "Oh, are you from Israel?" I tell them I'm not. I'm Lithuanian Jewish and my family has been in America for four generations. Lithuania is a small country bordering Poland.

I've always wanted to be able to say something more exotic about my background, like, "Funny you should ask: I'm part Dominican, part Danish, part Japanese, part Navajo, and part French." And I've always wanted to have a relative I'd never met before who was mysterious and performed great feats, someone I could admire and wonder about. Thanks to my dad's research, my fantasies don't seem so absurd anymore. Our family history may actually be more interesting and complicated than we knew.

"When I was younger my dad would always say that we were the only Brozgolds and I always found that impossible to believe," my dad said. "Now I know for sure it's not true."

My dad has been interested in genealogy for a long time, but only began to pursue this interest a few months ago. He does most of his research on the Internet, using search engines like Google. He types in various spellings of our last name and gets a list of United States residents with similar names. He then calls or e-mails the people he finds, tells them about his quest, and asks if they can give him any information.

Almost as soon as he began his research, he started turning up results. He quickly found some people who may be related to us through a name search on Google. We share a nearly identical last name, and can trace our ancestors back to the same province, but we haven't been able to establish a blood tie yet.

I'm constantly being updated on my dad's discoveries. Sometimes I come home for dinner after hanging out with friends and find him waiting to tell me a new exciting fact he's uncovered, such as a nephew we never knew about, or the port a relative's boat entered upon arrival in the U.S. at the turn of the century. Or he'll show me a picture a relative sent him, like a long-lost uncle who moved to China. "Hey!" he'll say. "Look at this! Can you see the resemblance?"

When I asked my dad what prompted him to start pursuing his genealogy, he reminded me of the time, about a year ago, when our dog Blanche got sick. My father took her to the vet, where she was diagnosed with cancer. "I was so upset because I thought: Oh, this poor dog, she doesn't even know where she came from," he recalled. "Which is so stupid because the dog doesn't care." But it made my dad realize that it was important to him to find out more about his own background.

My dad says he wants to claim his history. I shrug. Even though I'd like to have a more exciting story to tell about my ancestry, I have enough to worry about just starting my junior year of high school and planning out my future.

Even so, I appreciate what my dad's doing, not only because I see how happy it makes him, but because I know that he's doing it for me as well as himself. As his research progresses, I understand more and more how important family is. Sometimes just knowing that there are people out there with the same blood as you can be comforting. It's like having a tribe.

When I ask my dad how much he's found out, he replies, "Not much," but I think this is an understatement. For example, my father found out that

Sometimes just knowing that there are people out there with the same blood as you can be comforting.

we may have roots in Spain. He was completely wowed by this, and I was overjoyed. Finally, a little diversity in the family tree! The most important discovery so far, I feel, is the more concrete evidence of his research: actual people who may be related to us. Where our last name is Brozgold, theirs is Brozgol.

Alternative spellings of Jewish names are very common, because many Jews immigrating from European countries had their names misspelled when going through customs upon their arrival here. And that's not all. Recently, when my dad attended a high school graduation, he was surprised to hear a Brozgul called up to receive his diploma. My dad went up to him after the ceremony, met his parents, and told them about his research. Now they're supplying each other with information about their ancestors.

This chance meeting allowed me to see clearly, for the first time, the work my dad is doing. To me, research was something that had to do with numbers and science, two things I generally don't understand. But my dad's research is so different from that—he's researching people, not equations or earthworms. And it has the tangible impact of slowly making the world smaller and somehow more welcoming.

Though no sure family connections have been established, my father already feels like he's "part of a clan," as he puts it. When he says that, I too feel the pull of chromosomes, however slight, and of blood ties that are impossible to shake. Even if my dad can't trace our family tree back to its roots, and map out how our forefathers (and mothers) brought us into being, the whole thing will still have been worth the ride.

He has become, in my mind, a real father figure: the keeper of the family, the organizer of time.

He's re-established contact with people he hasn't spoken to in years, and he's also met new people who, even if they don't turn out to be family, may certainly become good friends. My dad's research has also allowed me to see him in a new light. I see his hopes and dreams, his desire to somehow bring everything together. He's going places, doing detective work, and discovering that it is a small world after all. He has become, in my mind, a real father figure: the keeper of the family, the organizer of time.

Hazak was 16 when he wrote this story. After high school, he went to Bennington College.

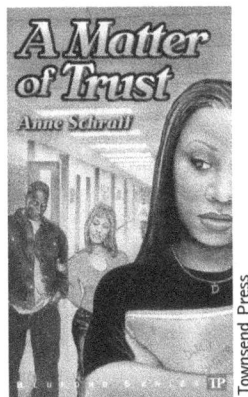

A Matter of Trust

Darcy Wills clenched her hands so hard that her fingernails dug into her palms. Hakeem Randall was walking to the front of the classroom to give his English report on *Macbeth*. He was a good student, but when he got nervous, he stuttered. Darcy dreaded this moment. She knew that if he began to stutter, the class would show no mercy. Just thinking about how embarrassed he would be made her cringe.

"Oh, Tarah," Darcy whispered to her friend, "I feel so *bad* for him!"

Tarah Carson turned a stern eye on Darcy, "Girl, he gotta fight this battle himself by doin' just what he's doin', facin' it."

Darcy had been dating Hakeem for just a few weeks, but at times it seemed that she had known him forever. He was a tall, handsome boy with a lot going for him—he was a good student,

---

Here's the first chapter from *A Matter of Trust*, by Anne Schraff, a novel about teens facing difficult situations like the ones you read about in this book. *A Matter of Trust* is one of several books in the Bluford Series™ by Townsend Press.

a great singer and guitar player, and a really nice person.

"My report on *Macbeth*," Hakeem began, "is about how g-g-guilt p-pplayed an important p-p-part in the story." Darcy's worst fears were coming true. She had never heard him stutter so badly. A soft ripple of laughter began in the back row and spread around the room.

Mr. Keenan, the teacher, glared at the students. "Let's try to remember this is tenth grade English, not second grade recess!" he growled. It did not help much. Hakeem struggled on with his report, stuttering often. Stifled giggles erupted throughout the room, gurgling like an underground spring. Roylin Bailey was making a big show of covering his mouth with both hands while he rocked back and forth.

" T-t-tomorrow, and t-t-tomorrow , and t-t-tomorrow," Hakeem stammered, "creeps in this p-p-petty p-p-pace from day to day—"

"Is 't-t-tomorrow' the same thing as 'tomorrow,' Mr. Keenan?" Roylin asked cruelly. "'Cause I want to know, sir."

Tarah's boyfriend, Cooper Hodden, just shook his head while other kids laughed. Cringing, Tarah shrank down in her seat. This was as hard for Hakeem's friends to watch as it was for Hakeem to endure, Darcy thought. Then, finally, mercifully, Hakeem's report was over, and he fled to his desk like a soldier racing across a battlefield and diving into a safe ditch.

Darcy reached over and covered Hakeem's hand with hers, whispering, "It was a good report."

Hakeem pulled his hand away, anger flaring in his usually warm eyes. "I made a fool of myself," he said bitterly.

Through the rest of the class, Hakeem sat staring at his desk and fiddling so violently with his pencil that he broke it in two. Darcy knew he was reliving the humiliation of the report. He told her once that he would replay his stuttering spells over and over in his mind. His speech therapist said there was nothing really wrong with him—it was something he would eventually overcome. But not today.

When the bell rang, Darcy hurried after Hakeem. "Hakeem, it wasn't that bad, really it wasn't!" she assured him.

Hakeem slammed his fist into his open palm and shook his head. "It was stupid! I'm stupid! If I wasn't stupid, I could talk right!"

"Hey man," Cooper said, standing in front of the snack machines, "don't sweat it. We all feel stupid sometimes. Once, I gave an oral presentation, and people were laughing but I didn't know why. Then the teacher whispered to me that my fly was unzipped."

"Yeah, and he was wearin' bright red boxer shorts that day," Tarah chimed in, smirking.

Hakeem jammed change into the soda-machine slot. He yanked out the can and walked away without saying anything. When Darcy tried to follow him, Tarah grabbed her wrist. "Girl," Tarah scolded, "give it a rest. We all got our lumps and bumps, and nobody gets outta this world without bein' banged up. It's not the end of the world that Hakeem messed up on a report. Let him work it out his own self."

Darcy reluctantly let Hakeem walk down the corridor alone. She felt so bad for him. Right now he was hating himself, and she understood that. Darcy had hated herself all through middle school and her first year at Bluford High because boys just seemed to ignore her. Every other girl in her class seemed prettier, more popular, and Darcy's shyness hurt something like Hakeem's stutter must have.

Darcy walked slowly towards the library to work on a science report. Her father had offered to take her to the Palomar Observatory for the report. The observatory would have made a great topic, but Darcy turned him down. Her father had been away from the family for five years, and now he was trying to rebuild his relationship with them. But Darcy felt awkward and strange with him.

Now she felt estranged from Hakeem too. He was hurting so much, and he would not let her try to help.

As Darcy reached the library, she noticed a flyer posted on the door:

Talent show auditions.
February 20, Noon.
Singers, musicians, dancers, artists.

The depressing thoughts of a moment ago were suddenly forgotten. Darcy's heart raced with excitement over what this could mean for Hakeem.

Everyone knew he was a great guitar player and a wonderful singer. When he sang, he never stuttered. Darcy could not wait till school was over so she could track him down. This show was just what he needed to boost his spirits.

After school, Darcy found Hakeem sitting under the pepper tree behind the Bluford parking lot. His guitar was resting on his lap. She sat beside him on the grass and said, "Did you hear about the auditions for the talent show? You'd be just great for that, Hakeem. You'd blow 'em away!"

"Yeah, watch the stuttering idiot perform. Maybe I could do a ventriloquist act so the kids'll think the dummy is the one who stutters!" Hakeem said bitterly.

"But you don't stutter when you sing," Darcy pointed out.

"I guess," he said, rolling a red berry between his fingers and watching the papery skin pop off, leaving a little brown seed. "Why don't *you* audition, Darcy? You have a nice singing voice. And you don't stutter."

"Oh, I'm no singer," Darcy blushed. " Sure you are," Hakeem insisted. "I've heard you. And you told me you used to sing in a church choir."

"But that's because Mom made me."

"Well, you should really enter this contest. It might give you that spark to start singing again."

"I will if you will," Darcy said impulsively, though the very thought of performing before the student body made her shudder.

Hakeem finally smiled. "Okay. Deal. Maybe we'll both make such fools of ourselves we'll have to run away to a desert island and hide."

Darcy glanced at her watch. A neighbor, Ms. Harris, was sitting with Darcy's grandmother, but Darcy still had to be home soon. "Gotta go now," she said. "Grandma will be needing me."

"How is she?" Hakeem asked.

Darcy shrugged. Grandma hadn't been well since her stroke a year and a half ago. "She's about the same. Some days, she's, you know, almost like normal for a few hours, and then she's back to thinking she's a little girl in her mom's house. I think she always knows me. I mean, she calls me 'Angelcake,' and she's always got a smile for me."

"Your parents getting any closer?" Hakeem asked.

"Dad goes down to the hospital where Mom works, and sometimes they talk in the cafeteria. I don't know if Mom would ever let him come back or even if he wants to. He's just trying to make up for what happened, you know, for running out on us."

"You want your parents together again, Darcy?"

"I don't know. Dad gets along good with Jamee. Even when we were little, she was always closer to him than I was. Maybe it's because she's two years younger than me, and Dad was always ready to baby her. I think right now she's ready to forgive him, but I can't say I am ready to do that. Maybe I should, but it's hard," Darcy admitted.

Hakeem gave Darcy a quick hug. "Like Tarah is always saying, 'We gotta make the best of what we got 'cause there ain't nothin' else to do!'"

They both laughed, and Hakeem picked up his guitar. He strummed a melody and began to sing in his rich, deep voice:

Will you hear me if I cry,
Above the thunder of anger,

Over blasts of fear and hate, When help comes not at all,
Or when it comes too late?
When streets explode with fire,
And hearts grow dead with grief,
When all the sounds are sad,
And there's no more relief?
Will you hear me if I cry?
Will you come before I die?

"Did you just write that?" Darcy asked.

"A couple of weeks ago. I was visiting my cousins, and we were talking about Russell Walker, that guy who went down in a drive-by shooting last year. I sort of wrote it for him."

"Yeah, I heard about him," Darcy said. "He was an honor student and an athlete, wasn't he?"

Hakeem nodded somberly.

"That was a crying shame," she added. "I hope they catch the guys who did it and put them behind bars for good."

Darcy was heading home when she ran into Brisana Meeks. Until just a few weeks ago, they had been best friends. When Darcy started hanging out with Tarah, Cooper and their friends, Brisana cut off the friendship. Since then, Darcy had made small efforts to repair their relationship. "Hey, Brisana," Darcy said, "how's it going?"

"Terrific," Brisana said with a sharp edge to her voice. Brisana had once told Darcy that she and Darcy were the bright, sophisticated kids at Bluford High. They were the "tens." It was their duty to avoid the low-class, stupid kids like Tarah and Cooper, who were zeroes.

"Want to go to the mall on Saturday, Brisana?" Darcy asked.

"With *you*?" Brisana scoffed, placing her hands on her hips. "No thanks," she added, leaving Darcy speechless.

As Darcy walked on, Roylin Bailey pulled up alongside her in a teal-blue Honda. "Hey Darcy, want a lift?" he shouted.

"No, thanks," Darcy said.

"Come on, Darcy," Roylin persisted. "Why are you wastin' your time with that stuttering fool? Sistah, I'm here to tell you, he ain't the one."

"Roylin, leave me alone. I don't remember asking for your opinion on my social life," Darcy snapped.

"Relax, girl. I'm just tryin' to help you out. You know, pass on the male perspective. And from where I'm sittin' you could do a lot better than Ha-ke-keke-keem," he said, snickering.

Out of the corner of her eye, Darcy saw Cooper Hodden's beat-up truck roll up behind the Honda. Tarah, sitting beside Cooper, yelled, "Cooper, baby, you know your brakes ain't so good. Don't go smashin' that Honda now!"

"I can't stop!" Cooper howled, hitting the horn and blasting Roylin's Honda out of his path. Both Cooper and Tarah doubled over laughing as Roylin sped away.

"You guys are outta your minds!" Darcy said, also laughing. "Thanks, I owe you." Leaning in the truck window, she confided, "Hey, guess what. I told Hakeem I'd sign up for the talent show that's coming up, just to make him try out. Problem is, I'm terrified of getting up in front of all those people. And then there's the issue of my voice."

"What's wrong with your voice?" Cooper asked. "You talkin' okay right now."

"No, my *singing* voice. It doesn't exactly make people jump to their feet with applause. Fall to their knees begging me to stop, maybe, but not jump to their feet," Darcy said.

"Girl, don't even worry about it," Tarah advised. "Just play the music real loud, smile real pretty, and nobody'll notice how you sing."

"Thanks, I'll keep that in mind," Darcy replied sarcastically.

Darcy climbed into the cramped front seat of the pickup truck for a ride home just as Hakeem sped by on a shiny silver motorbike. Hakeem did not seem to notice Darcy, but she saw him—with Brisana Meeks sitting behind him with her arms around his waist.

"That's weird," Darcy said. "I haven't even seen his new bike, and there she is riding on it."

"He prob'ly just givin' her a lift," Tarah said.

"Don't know about that," Cooper chimed in. "That girl's *fine*."

Tarah nudged Cooper in the ribs with her elbow, and he howled. But the damage was done. It was done the minute Darcy saw Brisana riding on Hakeem's motorbike.

"Brisana always used to make fun of Hakeem because he stuttered," Darcy said.

"Stuck-up girl like her, she prob'ly just going after him to mess with your head," Tarah replied.

Or maybe, Darcy thought, *I like Hakeem a lot more than he likes me*. A cold chill pressed down on Darcy's chest like a heavy blanket of ice.

Reprinted with permission from Townsend Press,
Copyright © 2002.

Teens:
How to Get More Out of This Book

Self-help: The teens who wrote the stories in this book did so because they hope that telling their stories will help readers who are facing similar challenges. They want you to know that you are not alone, and that taking specific steps can help you manage or overcome very difficult situations. They've done their best to be clear about the actions that worked for them so you can see if they'll work for you.

Writing: You can also use the book to improve your writing skills. Each teen in this book wrote 5-10 drafts of his or her story before it was published. If you read the stories closely you'll see that the teens work to include a beginning, a middle, and an end, and good scenes, description, dialogue, and anecdotes (little stories). To improve your writing, take a look at how these writers construct their stories. Try some of their techniques in your own writing.

Reading: Finally, you'll notice that we include the first chapter from a Bluford Series novel in this book, alongside the true stories by teens. We hope you'll like it enough to continue reading. The more you read, the more you'll strengthen your reading skills. Teens at Youth Communication like the Bluford novels because they explore themes similar to those in their own stories. Your school may already have the Bluford books. If not, you can order them online for only $1.

Resources on the Web

We will occasionally post Think About It questions on our website, www.youthcomm.org, to accompany stories in this and other Youth Communication books. We try out the questions with teens and post the ones they like best. Many teens report that writing answers to those questions in a journal is very helpful.

How to Use This Book in Staff Training

Staff say that reading these stories gives them greater insight into what teens are thinking and feeling, and new strategies for working with them. You can help the staff you work with by using these stories as case studies.

Select one story to read in the group, and ask staff to identify and discuss the main issue facing the teen. There may be disagreement about this, based on the background and experience of staff. That is fine. One point of the exercise is that teens have complex lives and needs. Adults can probably be more effective if they don't focus too narrowly and can see several dimensions of their clients.

Ask staff: What issues or feelings does the story provoke in them? What kind of help do they think the teen wants? What interventions are likely to be most promising? Least effective? Why? How would you build trust with the teen writer? How have other adults failed the teen, and how might that affect his or her willingness to accept help? What other resources would be helpful to this teen, such as peer support, a mentor, counseling, family therapy, etc?

Resources on the Web

From time to time we will post Think About It questions on our website, www.youthcomm.org, to accompany stories in this and other Youth Communication books. We try out the questions with teens and post the ones that they find most effective. We'll also post lesson for some of the stories. Adults can use the questions and lessons in workshops.

Teachers and Staff:
How to Use This Book in Groups

When working with teens individually or in groups, you can use these stories can help young people face difficult issues in a way that feels safe to them. That's because talking about the issues in the stories usually feels safer to teens than talking about those same issues in their own lives. Addressing issues through the stories allows for some personal distance; they hit close to home, but not too close. Talking about them opens up a safe place for reflection. As teens gain confidence talking about the issues in the stories, they usually become more comfortable talking about those issues in their own lives.

Below are general questions to guide your discussion. In most cases you can read a story and conduct a discussion in one 45-minute session. Teens are usually happy to read the stories aloud, with each teen reading a paragraph or two. (Allow teens to pass if they don't want to read.) It takes 10-15 minutes to read a story straight through. However, it is often more effective to let workshop participants make comments and discuss the story as you go along. The workshop leader may even want to annotate her copy of the story beforehand with key questions.

If teens read the story ahead of time or silently, it's good to break the ice with a few questions that get everyone on the same page: Who is the main character? How old is she? What happened to her? How did she respond? Another good starting question is: "What stood out for you in the story?" Go around the room and let each person briefly mention one thing.

Then move on to open-ended questions, which encourage participants to think more deeply about what the writers were feeling, the choices they faced, and they actions they took. There are no right or wrong answers to the open-ended questions.

Open-ended questions encourage participants to think about how the themes, emotions, and choices in the stories relate to their own lives. Here are some examples of open-ended questions that we have found to be effective. You can use variations of these questions with almost any story in this book.

—What main problem or challenge did the writer face?

—What choices did the teen have in trying to deal with the problem?

—Which way of dealing with the problem was most effective for the teen? Why?

—What strengths, skills, or resources did the teen use to address the challenge?

—If you were in the writer's shoes, what would you have done?

—What could adults have done better to help this young person?

—What have you learned by reading this story that you didn't know before?

—What, if anything, will you do differently after reading this story?

—What surprised you in this story?

—Do you have a different view of this issue, or see a different way of dealing with it, after reading this story? Why or why not?

Credits

The stories in this book originally appeared in the following Youth Communication publications:

"Father Lessons," by Otis Hampton, *Represent*, May/June 2009; "In An Octopus's Garden," by Dina Spanback, *New Youth Connections*, April 2008; "Suddenly, My Dad Is a Question Mark," by Natalie Kozakiewicz, *Represent*, May/June 2007; "How I Learned to Love My Stepdad," by Angelis Ulloa, *New Youth Connections*, June 1992; "'I Think These Drugs Are Daddy's,'" by Anonymous, *Represent*, September/October 2007; "Just the Two of Us,'" by Stephen Simpson, *New Youth Connections*, December 1998; "Hurting Myself for His Attention," by Natalie Olivero, *New Youth Connections*, November 2006; "Not My Idea of a Father," by Anonymous, *New Youth Connections*, May/June 1994; "Understanding Father's Love," by Chun Lar Tom, *New Youth Connections*, May/June 2002; "Not My Father's Daughter," by Sarvenaz Ezzati, *New Youth Connections*, September/October 1993; "Discovering My Dad at the Movies," by Daniela Castillo, *New Youth Connections*, November 2006; "The Guy I Call My Dad," by Anonymous, *New Youth Connections*, April 2001; "Long-Distance Dad," by Dahyana Orozco, *New Youth Connections*, November 2003; "Dealing With an Absent Dad," *Represent*, May/June 2009; "Invisible Man," by Onician Wood, *New Youth Connections*, January/February 2002; "Some POPS Are Hanging In," by Antwaun Garcia, *Represent*, March/April 2005; "Saying Goodbye to My Superman," by Griffin Kinard, *Represent*, September/October 2006; "My Father, My Friend," by Macario DeLaCruz, *New Youth Connections*, September/October 2001; "Meeting the Invisible Man," by Athena Karoutsos, *New Youth Connections*, May/June 2005; "Tracing My Family Tree," by Hazak Brozgold, *New Youth Connections*, November 2001.

About
Youth Communication

Youth Communication, founded in 1980, is a nonprofit youth development program located in New York City whose mission is to teach writing, journalism, and leadership skills. The teenagers we train become writers for our websites and books and for two print magazines: *New Youth Connections*, a general-interest youth magazine, and *Represent*, a magazine by and for young people in foster care.

Each year, up to 100 young people participate in Youth Communication's school-year and summer journalism workshops, where they work under the direction of full-time professional editors. Most are African-American, Latino, or Asian, and many are recent immigrants. The opportunity to reach their peers with accurate portrayals of their lives and important self-help information motivates the young writers to create powerful stories.

Our goal is to run a strong youth development program in which teens produce high quality stories that inform and inspire their peers. Doing so requires us to be sensitive to the complicated lives and emotions of the teen participants while also providing an intellectually rigorous experience. We achieve that goal in the writing/teaching/editing relationship, which is the core of our program.

Our teaching and editorial process begins with discussions

between adult editors and the teen staff. In those meetings, the teens and the editors work together to identify the most important issues in the teens' lives and to figure out how those issues can be turned into stories that will resonate with teen readers.

Once story topics are chosen, students begin the process of crafting their stories. For a personal story, that means revisiting events in one's past to understand their significance for the future. For a commentary, it means developing a logical and persuasive point of view. For a reported story, it means gathering information through research and interviews. Students look inward and outward as they try to make sense of their experiences and the world around them and find the points of intersection between personal and social concerns. That process can take a few weeks or a few months. Stories frequently go through ten or more drafts as students work under the guidance of their editors, the way any professional writer does.

Many of the students who walk through our doors have uneven skills, as a result of poor education, living under extremely stressful conditions, or coming from homes where English is a second language. Yet, to complete their stories, students must successfully perform a wide range of activities, including writing and rewriting, reading, discussion, reflection, research, interviewing, and typing. They must work as members of a team and they must accept individual responsibility. They learn to provide constructive criticism, and to accept it. They engage in explorations of truthfulness, fairness, and accuracy. They meet deadlines. They must develop the audacity to believe that they have something important to say and the humility to recognize that saying it well is not a process of instant gratification. Rather, it usually requires a long, hard struggle through many discussions and much rewriting.

It would be impossible to teach these skills and dispositions as separate, disconnected topics, like grammar, ethics, or assertiveness. However, we find that students make rapid progress when they are learning skills in the context of an inquiry that is personally significant to them and that will benefit their peers.

When teens publish their stories—in *New Youth Connections* and *Represent,* on the web, and in other publications—they reach tens of thousands of teen and adult readers. Teachers, counselors, social workers, and other adults circulate the stories to young people in their classes and out-of-school youth programs. Adults tell us that teens in their programs—including many who are ordinarily resistant to reading—clamor for the stories. Teen readers report that the stories give them information they can't get anywhere else, and inspire them to reflect on their lives and open lines of communication with adults.

Writers usually participate in our program for one semester, though some stay much longer. Years later, many of them report that working here was a turning point in their lives—that it helped them acquire the confidence and skills that they needed for success in college and careers. Scores of our graduates have overcome tremendous obstacles to become journalists, writers, and novelists. They include National Book Award finalist and MacArthur Fellowship winner Edwidge Danticat, novelist Ernesto Quinonez, writer Veronica Chambers, and *New York Times* reporter Rachel Swarns. Hundreds more are working in law, business, and other careers. Many are teachers, principals, and youth workers, and several have started nonprofit youth programs themselves and work as mentors—helping another generation of young people develop their skills and find their voices.

Youth Communication is a nonprofit educational corporation. Contributions are gratefully accepted and are tax deductible to the fullest extent of the law.

To make a contribution, or for information about our publications and programs, including our catalog of over 100 books and curricula for hard-to-reach teens, see www.youthcomm.org

About The Editors

Virginia Vitzthum is an editor at *Represent*, Youth Communication's magazine by and for teens in foster care. Before working at Youth Communication she wrote a book about Internet dating and a column for the Web magazine salon.com. She's also written for *Ms., Elle, the Village Voice, Time Out New York, Washington City Paper*, and other publications. She has edited law books, books about substance abuse treatment, and health care policy newsletters. She's written a play and a screenplay; produced several short videos; and volunteered at the 52nd St. Project, a children's theater, where she helped 9- to 11-year-olds write plays.

Keith Hefner co-founded Youth Communication in 1980 and has directed it ever since. He is the recipient of the Luther P. Jackson Education Award from the New York Association of Black Journalists and a MacArthur Fellowship. He was also a Revson Fellow at Columbia University.

Laura Longhine is the editorial director at Youth Communication. She edited *Represent*, Youth Communication's magazine by and for youth in foster care, for three years, and has written for a variety of publications. She has a BA in English from Tufts University and an MS in Journalism from Columbia University.

More Helpful Books
From Youth Communication

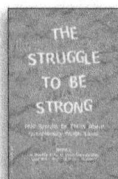

The Struggle to Be Strong: True Stories by Teens About Overcoming Tough Times. Foreword by Veronica Chambers. Help young people identify and build on their own strengths with 30 personal stories about resiliency. (Free Spirit)

Starting With "I": Personal Stories by Teenagers. "Who am I and who do I want to become?" Thirty-five stories examine this question through the lens of race, ethnicity, gender, sexuality, family, and more. Increase this book's value with the free Teacher's Guide, available from youthcomm.org. (Youth Communication)

Real Stories, Real Teens. Inspire teens to read and recognize their strengths with this collection of 26 true stories by teens. The young writers describe how they overcame significant challenges and stayed true to themselves. Also includes the first chapters from three novels in the Bluford Series. (Youth Communication)

The Courage to Be Yourself: True Stories by Teens About Cliques, Conflicts, and Overcoming Peer Pressure. In 26 first-person stories, teens write about their lives with searing honesty. These stories will inspire young readers to reflect on their own lives, work through their problems, and help them discover who they really are. (Free Spirit)

Out With It: Gay and Straight Teens Write About Homosexuality. Break stereotypes and provide support with this unflinching look at gay life from a teen's perspective. With a focus on urban youth, this book also includes several heterosexual teens' transformative experiences with gay peers. (Youth Communication)

Things Get Hectic: Teens Write About the Violence That Surrounds Them. Violence is commonplace in many teens' lives, be it bullying, gangs, dating, or family relationships. Hear the experiences of victims, perpetrators, and witnesses through more than 50 real-world stories. (Youth Communication)

From Dropout to Achiever: Teens Write About School. Help teens overcome the challenges of graduating, which may involve overcoming family problems, bouncing back from a bad semester, or even dropping out for a time. These teens show how they achieve academic success. (Youth Communication)

My Secret Addiction: Teens Write About Cutting. These true accounts of cutting, or self-mutilation, offer a window into the personal and family situations that lead to this secret habit, and show how teens can get the help they need. (Youth Communication)

Sticks and Stones: Teens Write About Bullying. Shed light on bullying, as told from the perspectives of the bully, the victim, and the witness. These stories show why bullying occurs, the harm it causes, and how it might be prevented. (Youth Communication)

Boys to Men: Teens Write About Becoming a Man. The young men in this book write about confronting the challenges of growing up. Their honesty and courage make them role models for teens who are bombarded with contradictory messages about what it means to be a man. (Youth Communication)

The Fury Inside: Teens Write About Anger. Help teens manage their anger. These writers show how they got better control of their emotions and sought the support of others. (Youth Communication)

To order these and other books, go to:
www.youthcomm.org
or call 212-279-0708 x115

www.ingramcontent.com/pod-product-compliance
Lightning Source LLC
Chambersburg PA
CBHW051727090426
42738CB00010B/2133